INSIDE

IRELAND

Phoenix Park, Dublin

INSIDE IRELAND

EILÍS DILLON

PHOTOGRAPHS BY TOM KENNEDY

HODDER AND STOUGHTON
LONDON SYDNEY AUCKLAND TORONTO

To Honor

British Library Cataloguing in Publication Data

Dillon, Eilís
Inside Ireland
1. Ireland – Pictorial works
I. Title   II. Kennedy, Tom
941.508′24′022   DA980

ISBN 0 340 26342 3

Printed in Great Britain
for Hodder and Stoughton Limited,
Mill Road, Dunton Green, Sevenoaks, Kent
by The Pitman Press, Bath

Designed by Trevor Vincent

Photoset by Rowland Phototypesetting Ltd,
Bury St Edmunds, Suffolk.

Hodder and Stoughton Editorial Office:
47 Bedford Square, London WC1B 3DP

From the Hill of Tara

ONE

W̅HEN my parents first became interested in each other, about 1912, they had no idea that Plunketts and Dillons had been intermarrying for more than five hundred years. Both families had come with the Anglo-Norman invasion of Ireland in the late twelfth century. Some say the Plunketts came earlier and were Danes. After the first battles had decided that they were to stay, they settled down close to their Irish neighbours in what passed for peace in those days, becoming 'more Irish than the Irish themselves'. Or so it is said. In fact they had a great degree of confidence in their ability as leaders of opinion, with little of the introspection and uneasiness of the Celts. They built high, impregnable castles, so strong that some of them are made habitable from time to time, to this day. From up there on the battlements they saw which was the best land and became its owners by every means. Later they arranged marriages among themselves, consolidating their gains, and built large mansions, laid out gardens and considered themselves as part of the aristocracy.

I remember my amazement when I first discovered the names of my collateral ancestors in school history books; one hanged, drawn and quartered at Tyburn, many imprisoned and exiled for rebelling against the Crown, one executed by firing squad for the same crime only four years before I was born. Naturally it became necessary to find out how and why these things happened to people who were presumably rather like my parents, my uncles and my grandparents, all of whom had endangered their lives in the same way. One can't very well put off people who ask, 'Was that your uncle who signed the proclamation of the Irish Republic and was shot within a week?' Or I would be asked if I was related to John Blake Dillon of the 1848 Rising, or to Blessed – now Saint – Oliver Plunkett. In the Ireland of my youth, the admission that I was indeed related to all of these interesting people met with an occasional raised eyebrow. Young people of our class were warned that we were dangerous company, but while the family record shows that it was quite dangerous to be either a Dillon or a Plunkett, it was never too dangerous to know them.

They were not always rebels. In the seventeenth century, Wentworth Dillon, fourth Earl of Roscommon, was a poet of considerable standing, translating Horace's *Ars*

Emo House, County Laois

Kilkea Castle, County Kildare

Poetica into verse and also writing a long treatise in verse, which is still entertaining and useful, on the translation of poetry. He was educated at Caen but brought up a Protestant, and may have been an example of the custom of electing one member of a great family to adopt the Reformation so as to hold on to the family possessions.

The Plunketts followed the same custom. At the time of the dissolution of the monasteries, one Richard Plunkett was Abbot of Kells in County Meath. A family story tells that he gave up all of the monastery property on November 18th, 1539, but held back the celebrated illuminated copy of the four Gospels known as the *Book of Kells*. The book passed from one Plunkett house to another, hotly pursued by someone in authority who knew about it and was determined to have it. Its last Plunkett refuge was with Gerald Plunkett of Dublin, who passed it on to Archbishop Ussher, but it did not reach Trinity College until five years after the archbishop's death when a part of his library was acquired by the College. The *Book of Kells* is guarded by a special custodian who never takes his eye off it so long as the library is open.

The family solidarity which showed in their care for the *Book of Kells* was a reflection of their attitude towards each other. When their cousin Oliver became Archbishop of Armagh and Primate of Ireland in 1670 the family, as he put it, 'vied with each other in seeing which of them should receive me into his house'. By 1679 the persecution of Catholics had reached such a pitch that Oliver was a dangerous visitor, but still his cousins sheltered him on many occasions and took care of his vestments and Mass vessels, articles that anyone less confident would rather not have had about the house. They were not able to prevent his arrest and horrible end, however, but their concern for him and pride in him may be judged by the fact that they carefully preserved those same vestments and vessels, until the present Lord Fingall sold them to the Catholic bishop of Meath in the 1950s. Branches of the family from all over Europe were represented at Oliver's canonisation in Rome, in 1976.

The Plunketts rarely became professional fighting men, but the Dillons fought for King James against William of Orange. After the siege of Limerick, in 1690, when the Irish aristocracy were exiled with their regiments, the Dillons took a regiment to France. The Irish got a splendid welcome at the court of Versailles and in due course the Dillons, as well as the other Norman families, had their ancient French titles restored to them. They entered the service of France *en bloc*, in the manner of the times, but at first with a strong idea of returning to Ireland and retaking their castles and mansions and restoring the old way of life. The Dillons' main castle, Portlick, is still to be seen near Lough Ree, and it must have been a sore thing to leave such splendour behind.

These *émigré* families, Sheldons, Brownes, Lallys, Rothes, Dillons, fought in every country in Europe and in their colonies, many of them dying on foreign battlefields, and perhaps echoing the sentiment 'Oh, that this were for Ireland!' voiced by Patrick Sarsfield, Earl of Lucan, as he perished on the battlefield of Landen.

In the nineteenth century, when Thomas Davis was doing everything he could to arouse Irish nationalism, he composed a number of ballads about these unfortunate aristocrats. 'Clare's Dragoons' goes to a rousing air and has bloodthirsty lines:

> *So fling your green flag to the sky,*
> *Let Limerick be your battle cry,*
> *And charge till blood flows fetlock high*
> *Around the track of Clare's Dragoons.*

Another says mournfully:

> *On far, foreign fields, from Dunkirk to Belgrade*
> *Lie the soldiers and chiefs of the Irish Brigade.*

This was parodied in the anti-recruiting campaign of 1917 to a grimmer second line, designed to syphon off the romantic element:

> *On far foreign fields from Dunkirk to Belgrade*
> *Lie the shoulders and shins of the Irish Brigade.*

When I was a child, names that had been Englished as Browne, Power, Burke were transferred back to their older forms in Irish and became de Brún, de Paor, de Búrca, much nearer to the original French. We, however, became Diolún, with the accent on the second syllable. Recently I discovered the reason for this: that our name, de Lion (lion showing boldly on the crest) was pronounced de Lioune in France until the seventeenth century. I have no idea when the characteristic *de* was dropped, but Dillon they remained throughout their time in France, and so the name remains there still.

In eighteenth-century Ireland, Catholics were barred from all education, but families like the Dillons and Plunketts set up illegal schools in the upper floors of their houses, with a resident schoolmaster, and they also employed travelling schoolmasters, specialists in Latin, French, mathematics, Greek, music, dancing. Children from the neighbouring houses were invited to attend. Each of the travelling teachers stayed for a while in the house and taught his own subject exclusively. This custom continued long after Catholic education was permitted in some measure, after 1782. My mother told me that her grandfather, Walter Plunkett of the Fingall branch, said it was very strange to concentrate on French for several weeks and then to drop it suddenly and switch to mathematics or the piano. However odd the system may seem to us now, the children were well educated at home, and numbers of them later went to one or other of the Irish Colleges in Europe to complete their studies.

These schools were by no means hedge schools. Some of the travelling schoolmasters were priests and had to be carefully hidden from the eye of the authorities. In the early eighteenth century a bounty was paid for the head of a priest or a wolf, and later, according to the historian Lecky, it was proposed by a member of the Dublin Parliament that any priest caught in Ireland should be castrated. There is no record of this having been done, but it must have made everyone very nervous.

The Irish Colleges in Europe were at Bordeaux, Paris, St. Omer, Louvain, Douai, Salamanca and Rome. Some had medical schools, notably Bordeaux which had the honour of producing Dr. Guillotin who invented the machine named after him. Execution by the axe was apparently much nastier. One of the sources of revenue for the Bordeaux College was for a time grave-digging by the students, a lugubrious task for boys who had survived a perilous sea journey in small sailing-ships. This was commented on eventually by someone in authority and a subsidy provided instead.

The American War of Independence and the French Revolution caused great excitement in Ireland, especially among the Protestant aristocracy. Many of them had never accepted their position as colonists. By the end of the eighteenth century they regarded Ireland as their native land and they were tired of being treated as second-class citizens when they went to England. After all, it was their ancestors who had fought with fire and sword to exterminate as many as possible of the Irish for the comfort and benefit of England, and now they found themselves being referred to as 'Wild Irish'. Too many decisions of their exclusively Protestant Parliament could be and were reversed by Westminster. There was an uncomfortable little furore when no places were provided for the Irish peeresses at the coronation of George III, and rude jokes were made about their accents. Many of them still retained the vocabulary and pronunciation of Queen Elizabeth's time, and do to this day, notably an 'aw' sound instead of an 'ah.'

Apart from personal humiliations they objected to the neglect of Ireland's great economic possibilities, and when England was busy with the American War they demanded free trade in no uncertain terms. Until then, these loyal subjects of the Crown were continually suffering financial set-backs from a policy which seemed very sensible to the Westminster Parliament. If trade in wool, linen, hides or any other basic export was not doing well in England, Ireland was forbidden to export at all until things looked up. After free trade was granted in 1782 Ireland became extraordinarily prosperous, and the local Parliament in Dublin began to lift its head and became more and more independent.

In Dublin a programme of public building had begun in the seventeenth century and was continued now with enthusiasm. The Custom House and the Four Courts date from this period and were worthy successors of the Royal Hospital in Kilmainham, the Parliament House, now the Bank of Ireland, and Trinity College. The King's Inns was begun and the Royal Exchange, now the City Hall, was finished. In 1769 a competition had brought to Dublin two English architects specialising in large buildings, Thomas Cooley and James Gandon, while at the same time the sixth Lord Fitzwilliam began a scheme of development south of the river which continued for a hundred years, providing broad streets and large, well-built private houses over a wide area between the Liffey and the Dodder rivers.

No Catholic could be a Member of Parliament and though the Protestants formed only ten per cent of the total population they had no intention of giving votes to the Catholics or allowing them to enter the professions or the army, except as privates, and even that was a new concession. As the country prospered, this prohibition had the curious effect of sending the Catholics into business, especially money-lending, in which trade they often found their masters in their power. It had long been considered respectable in Ireland to be in trade, and as some of the businessmen became increasingly rich it became more and more difficult to hold the line between Catholic and Protestant.

A small number of Protestants deplored the injustice of the prohibitions against their Catholic neighbours and tried by argument and persuasion to change the system, without success. Even Henry Grattan, who was held in great esteem and was the leader of the House, lamented all his life that in spite of his best efforts he was prevented by his colleagues from benefiting ninety per cent of the people of his country. Gradually a movement grew up in favour of Catholic emancipation, largely through the work of Protestants, but success was still a long way off.

A concession to the Catholics in 1795 was the foundation of Maynooth College for the education of priests. The idea of educating Catholic priests in Ireland had caused great alarm, but it was no secret that the main object was to keep the students away from the dangerous, new-fangled ideas of liberty, equality and fraternity then rife in France.

A curious story has gained credence over the years that the conservative, not to say rigid, view of Catholicism observable in Ireland is caused by the Jansenist leanings of the French professors who staffed the College from its foundation. In fact, everyone appointed at Maynooth was obliged to take an oath against Jansenism, which was regarded as a dangerous philosophy, but in any case there were very few Frenchmen on the faculty, only two or three, and these left within a few years because they were unhappy in Ireland and particularly in Maynooth. It is true that the Irish professors had been educated in France, but their sympathy with the standards of France may be gauged by the fact that they teased the French professors unmercifully for their hide-bound ways, and contributed to their quick departure. One of their most ill-mannered pranks was to hold a long conversation in a gibberish which they said was Gaelic, and drown out the French who wished their language to become that of the College.

A more likely explanation of Irish conservatism may be found in the national temperament which does not like change, and clings closely to tradition in everything, or perhaps in the determination to avoid erosion of the Irish way of life. Another probable reason is that, during the long period when they were forbidden to hold religious services, the Catholics had to resort to pious practices to keep their faith alive. This created a kind of lay or family theologian who is a menace to any religious structure.

In 1798, three years after the foundation of Maynooth College, a popular uprising inspired by the French Revolution and the American War of Independence was put down with a savagery remarkable even for that period. The leaders were educated people, northern Presbyterians and southern Catholics with a sprinkling of Protestants, all united in a manner that seems like a dream now. Since then they have scarcely ever agreed on a common cause. The leaders were executed, the rank and file slaughtered on the field or hanged in hundreds, one by one, on travelling gallows, like the French with their travelling guillotine. In Wexford the ill-disciplined rebels became a mob and committed atrocities equal to those they suffered themselves, though on a smaller scale as befitted the losers. The sites of these massacres are still remembered throughout the country.

One of the leaders in Wexford, about whom a ballad is still sung, was Father Murphy who had been educated at Bordeaux Irish College. He was driven to rebellion when he saw that the Catholics were first ordered to give up their arms and bring them to their churches, then were set upon and murdered indiscriminately. The burning of his own church decided him that he must put up some defence. The whole affair makes grisly reading. Two years later the country was deprived of its Parliament by the Act of Union.

Wexford

The Irish Parliament voted itself out of office, its members bribed by the Lord Chancellor with titles and with sums of money which, as he said, were larger than had ever been spent on bribes in Ireland before. Union had been discussed for a long time as a last resort and it should also be remembered that the Protestant aristocracy was in a state of shock at the fate of some of their co-religionists, who had been tortured and killed with a fervour and ferocity usually reserved for Catholics. One of them recorded that the sight of a *gentleman*'s head spiked outside Dublin Castle made him a loyalist for life. That was the object. Among the common people rebellion smouldered, fed by ballads and memories transmitted from father to son, some of them in the Irish language which was largely unknown to the powers in Dublin.

In that fatal year of 1798 a William Plunkett, a barrister and Member of Parliament, pledged his support to the Irish Parliament for the Government's exceptional measures against the rebels. Later, oddly enough, with John Philpot Curran he defended the Sheares brothers for their part in the rebellion but was not successful in freeing them. William Plunkett later became Lord Plunkett as a result of being made Irish Lord Chancellor in the Westminster Parliament. His cousin James Plunkett was the rebel Wolfe Tone's friend and organiser in Galway and Mayo, and Tone remarks early in his diary that Plunkett is going to convert Lord Dillon to the nationalist cause. They were probably related to each other by marriage.

Catholic emancipation was finally achieved in 1829, a date I am not likely to forget because its centenary was celebrated with bands and processions and outdoor religious services in 1929, when I was nine years old. Daniel O'Connell was chiefly responsible for the passing of the Bill and, encouraged by his success, he travelled throughout the country urging the people to use their new power to demand the repeal of the Act of Union. A barrister, a loud and effective speaker, once seen and heard he was never forgotten. His family home in Kerry was run in the old Irish way, with dozens of relations always coming and going, twenty or thirty people sitting down to meals together every day, to the astonishment of foreign visitors. Stories about him were handed on from generation to generation until he developed into the traditional hero of folklore, even to having some of the stories told in rhyme. One of these concerns an alleged attempt to poison him at a banquet in London. The plot became known to one of the maids who was to serve the meal and she warned him, in the following dialogue, that his wine was poisoned:

THE GIRL   *A Dhomhnaill Uí Chonaill, an dtuigeann tú Gaeilge?*
(Daniel O'Connell, do you understand Irish?)

16

O'Connell	*Tuigim go maith, a chailín ó Éirinn.* (I understand very well, girl from Ireland.)
The girl	*Ith do dhóithin, ach ná h-ól éinní –* *Tá salann id phraisigh ó aréir duit.* (Eat plenty but don't drink anything – There is salt in your porridge since last night.)

Note that she calls him simply 'Daniel O'Connell' without a preliminary title. In the same way the saints are simply Patrick, Brigid, Colmcille, Ciarán.

Not all of the folklore is savoury. I have heard it said that one could not throw a stone over a workhouse wall without striking one of Daniel O'Connell's bastards. There is a sort of grudging admiration of his prowess in the accusation, but there is no proof that there was any truth in it.

It must have been agonisingly difficult to be the saviour of such a down-and-out people as the Irish were then, after more than a century of oppression. They never forgot him. Throughout the country one is shown Repeal Rocks, natural platforms from which he made his speeches for the repeal of the Act of Union, but I have heard him being blamed bitterly for urging the people to drop their ancient language in favour of English and for not having got Catholic emancipation for the whole population, only for those who had a certain property qualification. It has also been said of him that he caused the great famine of 1845–47. Two years before, in 1843, he dispersed a huge and militant meeting of almost destitute men from every part of Ireland, assembled at Clontarf on the outskirts of Dublin, and advised them to go peacefully home. His critics say that, if he had encouraged them then to fight for their rights, they would have seized the food which was being exported throughout those terrible famine years, instead of letting themselves be starved to death or shipped off like cattle on unseaworthy vessels to Canada and America.

Cecil Woodham-Smith, however, in her book *The Great Hunger*, proves pretty conclusively that an army of beggars could not possibly have stood up to the military detachments which escorted the grain and other food to the ports. She describes one occasion on which it was attempted, and the resulting massacre. O'Connell was shocked by the bloodshed he had seen in France during the French Revolution, when he was a student, and the fearful tales that reached him in Dublin in 1798 before he fled home to safety in Kerry. By 1845 he had passed the age when one yells slogans to send unarmed peasants into battle.

Dublin dusk

Heartbroken by the famine, O'Connell died in 1847, in Genoa, on his way to Rome. I have seen a plaque on a house wall there, commemorating him as 'Danieli Oconnello'. With a marvellous unconcern for the trouble he was causing, he bequeathed his heart to Rome where it is now encased in a marble tomb set into the wall in a corridor in the Irish College, and his body to Ireland where it rests under a monument in the form of a round tower, visible from a long distance, in Glasnevin cemetery in Dublin. Dublin's large, beautiful main street is named after him, and his statue at one end faces the river Liffey. The Dublin people, with their typical brand of humour, name the four figures at the base Faith, Hope, Charity and Mrs. O'Connell.

In his excellent biography of O'Connell, Seán O'Faoláin sums up what he gave us as the principle of life as a democracy. This is indeed true but I think he also gave us a breath of strong country air in the capital, noticeable to this day.

In the middle of the nineteenth century the Catholic Plunketts began to move to Dublin and take advantage of the possibilities of trade. It was still a little city, bounded more or less by the canals that had been built in the eighteenth century. The Georgian squares and long, straight streets had grown, north and south of the river. My great-grandfather, Patrick Plunkett, came up from Killeen in 1844, after the death of his father, Walter. They belonged to the Fingall branch and Walter had just been buried in the family chapel, where twenty years earlier his father, George, had been laid to rest.

Patrick Plunkett often talked to my mother about his youth in Meath. He lived to be ninety-one – his father had lived to a hundred and three – and at the end of his life he showed my mother a scar on his head and described how he had acquired it. The deer on the Fingall estate had a habit of roaming at night through the tilled fields of the farm, and one night Patrick went with a large knife to kill the next one that came through the gap they had made for themselves in the hedge. The deer was also armed, however, with a wicked pair of horns and Patrick was glad to escape with nothing more than the scars which he carried for the rest of his life.

My grandfather was born in Aungier Street, the third child of Patrick and Elizabeth Plunkett, on December 3rd, 1851. He was named George Noble, the latter from his mother's maiden name, and always used both names, giving rise later to a strange misconception in the minds of some that the 'Noble' was part of his title. A family story goes that on the night of his birth two men happened to visit the house and, on hearing that there was a new-born baby, they asked to see him. Each of them in turn took him in his arms and one of them said, 'Now this child can always say that the big drummer and the little drummer of Vinegar Hill held him in their arms as an infant.'

Fifty-four years before, in 1798, Vinegar Hill in Wexford was the scene of the last battle of the rebellion, when General Lake surrounded twenty thousand wretched rebels on the top of the hill and would have massacred them all if a gap had not inadvertently been left through which many of them escaped. The biblical scene with the baby was a sign that rebellion had only been driven underground. Three years before my grandfather's birth, in 1848, there had been a failed attempt at another uprising but it must have raised hopes in the old warriors that they would some day see one succeed. This story is the only evidence I have heard that there were drummers at Vinegar Hill.

Patrick Plunkett prospered and presently went into business as a builder, in partnership with his cousin Patrick Cranny who was also in the leather and shoemaking business. My grandmother once told me that they were assisted by the Protestant Plunkett cousins in getting the concession to build on the valuable Pembroke estate, which covered a large part of the southern suburbs of the city.

The Pembroke leases were devised in England and make strange reading. The type of buyer considered desirable was clearly stated, and persons who followed certain trades were excluded. One was that of 'night man', whose job it was to call at city houses by night and take away the day's slops. English architects designed the brick houses on the Pembroke estate and it was specified that certain English materials were to be imported and used.

One of the partners' first ventures was Palmerston Road, a long, elegant street of large town houses. They planted trees on the footpaths, an innovation in those days which they copied on most of their other streets. Patrick Plunkett had bought the land from Sir John Purser Griffith and it included what is now Palmerston Park, Cowper Road and Belgrave Road. Some of this land had been the scene of the battle of Rathmines in 1649, between the forces of the Marquess of Ormonde and the loyalist garrison of Dublin. It was still known then as 'the bloody fields', and when excavations were made for the buildings, bones of horses and men were frequently turned up.

Some years later when my great-grandfather went to live on Palmerston Road, he kept a large piece of ground with his own house, a tennis court at one end and stables for all his horses at the other. An odd patch intervened between these two sections because the lease ordained that the amenities of the Reverend Mr. Johnson must not be interfered with. There was no boundary, and no one remembers who Mr. Johnson was or whether he enjoyed his oddly-shaped garden, but that patch remained vacant until quite recently when someone built on it, presumably without title.

Victorian Dublin town houses

Over the next years the partners built Belgrave Road, Elgin Road, Wellington Road, Clyde Road, Raglan Road, Marlborough Road and Eglinton Road, many of their streets being on the Pembroke estate and some on land that they had bought for themselves. By this time they had covered a large part of Rathmines and Donnybrook. Patrick Cranny built himself a fine house off Marlborough Road and named it Muckross Park in memory of his Kerry connections. His son Gerald was by this time an architect, and he designed this house and also those on Marlborough Road. Patrick Plunkett went to live first on Belgrave Road and then at 14 Palmerston Road, moving his family from Aungier Street in 1854. Diseases of all kinds, lumped under the generic name of famine fever, raged throughout the country and no doubt it seemed like good sense to leave Aungier Street for an airier situation.

With leave to build was given an instruction that the new streets were to be named after great Englishmen. My great-grandfathers – as they turned out to be – amused themselves by choosing some names which were causing embarrassment to the Empire at the time, but few people besides themselves saw the joke. Lord Elgin had been much criticised for levering off some of the frieze of the Parthenon and taking it – not very efficiently – back to England, where it is still to be seen in the British Museum. His excuse was that the Turks were going to destroy it anyway by using it for target practice, but Elgin was roundly condemned as a vandal and his stock was low. Lord Raglan had just been discovered to have allowed dislike of his colleague, Lord Lucan, to affect his decisions in the Crimean War, with disastrous effects.

My grandfather was three years old when his father moved to Belgrave Road in 1854. The country was once more seething with rebellion. Soon after the move, my grand-father was playing in the garden of the new house all alone, when two men leaped over the wall, approached him quickly and asked him if the soldiers had come by. He replied that they had not. The men asked him to tell the soldiers, if they came, that he had seen them and that they had gone towards the country. They then left him, climbing the wall and going in the direction of the city. Within a few minutes a troop of soldiers appeared and questioned this precocious child, asking if he had seen two men run by. He replied that he had indeed seen them, and that they had gone towards the country, whereupon the soldiers hurried off in the wrong direction and my grandfather went back to his play, with a feeling of great satisfaction.

In recounting this story he said that his thoughts were perfectly clear. He already knew, at that tender age, that the fleeing men were Irish patriots and that they were not to be betrayed to their pursuers.

It seems likely that what he had heard was family talk. The Plunketts were law-abiding people, but Patrick had many times witnessed in Meath the failure of the police to protect the Catholics in the aftermath of the Orange procession to commemorate the battle of the Boyne. As has happened in our time, late in the evening things got out of hand and a mob of loyalists would attack the Catholics. Patrick Plunkett told my mother that he had seen these victims crawling down to a stream for a drink in the early morning, having hidden all night from their tormentors, while a crowd of Orange women waited behind the bushes 'to beat their brains out with stones'. Patrick's father had heard details of the French Revolution discussed at home by his parents, and he brought up his family not to believe in violence, but no thinking man could disregard the condition of the poor at that time.

Even rich Catholics were expected to keep a low profile. The Plunketts thought well of themselves and Patrick wished to take part in local affairs. Rathmines did not yet have a town hall and the town council had fallen into the habit of meeting in the vestry of the Protestant church after Sunday service. Wearying of this exclusiveness, one Sunday Patrick and his cousin and partner Patrick Cranny took their long builders' ladders, climbed into the vestry by the window and were seated at the table, waiting, when the service was over and the council assembled. After that, meetings moved to a more public place.

Patrick and Elizabeth Plunkett's two older children died in childhood. Once, when he was an old man, on one of their birthdays my grandfather spoke to me of his brother with tears in his eyes, mentioning a beautiful flowered cotton pinafore that he had worn. His mother became increasingly dispirited as her children died, and she rightly attributed it to the diseases that were still ravaging the country. These were mainly typhoid and tuberculosis, which carried off adults and children of every class. In 1857, when he was six years old, she decided that the only hope for her remaining son was to get him out of the country, and so she settled him in the Jesuit school in Nice, which was said to have the most salubrious climate in Europe. It was still Italian-speaking, still named Nizza, and was at that time a possession of Sardinia. A plebiscite in 1860 restored it to France.

There my grandfather remained, spending his summers in San Remo, until he was twelve years old. It was there that he learned both French and Italian well, and sowed the seeds of his lifelong love of Italian painting. In 1863 his life was thought to be out of danger and he was taken home to Ireland.

Sandymount Strand

TWO

❧

DUBLIN in the nineteenth century was simply a part of England. There was a Lord Lieutenant who kept something like the state of a king, with an entourage and levees and drawing-rooms on the social side, and large numbers of English-born civil servants on the administrative side. A great many English companies, from shoe and grocery stores to insurance companies, had branches in Ireland and almost all of them had English managers. Most of these people lived in hopes of returning to better jobs in England but in any case of retiring there. There was a constant demand for good houses to rent. The Plunkett and Cranny partners sold some of theirs, but they kept a great many and lived on the rents. They never had trouble finding tenants, especially as Patrick Cranny's son Gerald had thoughtfully included bathrooms in those houses that he designed – the first bathrooms in Dublin, according to family tradition. True or false, the statement in itself is a proof of their awareness that they were building a new world.

Gradually they became experts in their new business, though they often found it exasperating. There could be no doubt of this in the mind of anyone who has heard them pronounce the word 'tenants' with a powerful emphasis on the first syllable.

Dublin was not a popular capital with the rest of the country and sometimes seems to have remained unpopular to this day. One can easily understand why. It was the centre of the old Pale, a kind of early partition of Ireland set up by the Normans, or even by the Danes, and all kinds of uncomfortable and oppressive laws had been issued from it so often that the rest of Ireland regarded Dublin Castle as a symbol of the power of the invaders. Folk-songs in Irish commemorate the fact that anyone wearing Irish dress or with an Irish hair-style was not allowed within the walls of Dublin. The double life of the city is best exemplified by the fact that its name in Irish, *Baile Átha Cliath*, means the town of the ford of the hurdles, and bears no resemblance to the name it was given by the Danes.

Nevertheless Dublin has produced a tough proletariat of a kind only to be found in capital cities, indomitable, humorous and with a strong sense of its own history. The centre for these people is the area still known as the Liberties, because in medieval times it was not under the jurisdiction of the city but owed allegiance to the Archbishops of

Dublin or to the Earls of Meath, on whose property they lived. Their territory stretches between St. Patrick's Cathedral and the river. It is the oldest part of the city, where some of the most interesting and important buildings are to be found. Here was the Viking settlement, in the middle of the ninth century, from which useful raids could be conducted inland or across the Channel to England, or even as far as Normandy.

As any Dubliner will tell you, the Danes were defeated by King Brian Boru in a decisive battle at Clontarf in 1014. They never regained their power. They lived on in Dublin, however, trading and going to sea, and intermarrying with the Irish, but one may gauge the difficulty of their position from the boasting of the victors which has continued without intermission for almost a thousand years. Once in a Dublin bar I heard shouts of anger and a moment later a furious customer was being bundled outside by his friends to cool off in the winter night air. He had become involved in an argument with a Danish tourist, and as he left the company he yelled over and over, 'We drowned them in the Tolka in 1014!' Checking the details of the battle, which are recorded with great dramatic sorrow in the Norse sagas, I found that the Irish did indeed drown the Danes in the Tolka river, now a muddy tidal stream on the north side of the city. In mitigation of the Irish boasting it must be said that they rarely won a battle in the ensuing thousand years.

The most notable incumbent of St. Patrick's Cathedral was Dean Swift, who also founded St. Patrick's Hospital for psychiatric disorders. His cathedral contains his tomb, with the Latin epitaph that he composed himself. This was loosely translated by Yeats, but a prose translation would better keep the strength of the original:

> HERE LIES THE BODY OF JONATHAN SWIFT, D.D.,
> DEAN OF THIS CATHEDRAL,
> WHERE SAVAGE INDIGNATION CAN
> LACERATE HIS HEART NO MORE.
> GO, TRAVELLER, AND IMITATE, IF YOU CAN,
> ONE WHO NEVER SPARED HIMSELF IN
> THE VIGOROUS DEFENCE OF LIBERTY.

Folklore still exists concerning Swift – tales of his wit, of his political pamphlets and his love affairs. Some say he haunts the cathedral, but he would probably consider this beneath his dignity.

Marsh's Library, close by, is also said to be haunted. The building was begun by Archbishop Narcissus Marsh in 1702, to the design of an architect named Robinson who also built the Royal Hospital at Kilmainham. The library is a small building with the books arranged in bays. These now have wire-mesh fronts to them, and by an old regulation the librarian is obliged to lock the reader in, to safeguard the books. The story goes that the first Librarian's daughter eloped, leaving a letter to her father explaining her action, and placing it between the leaves of one of the books which she expected him to read. For one reason or another he never found it, and she forgot which book it was, and so she still flutters through the library by night, opening one book after another in the hope of discovering its whereabouts. Presumably one would have to be forgotten by the librarian, and spend the night in the cage to see this unfortunate young lady at work.

A number of ghosts should have the privilege of haunting Dublin Castle. It still has evil associations in the minds of Dubliners – heads spiked above the gate after many uprisings; the wife of one of the O'Neill kings suspended in a cage, in view of all, to starve, in retaliation for her husband's insubordination; in my own lifetime the centre from which the Black and Tans went out on their nightly rampages through the city. Restored now, it begins to have a pleasanter character and is used for harmless purposes – banquets and conferences – and to house among other things the Genea-logical Office with its little museum of heraldry.

Facing down Dame Street with its back to Trinity College, a statue of King William of Orange was erected in 1701. It was repeatedly assaulted by the people of the Liberties and by the students of Trinity College, who successively painted it black, took off its head, removed its sceptre and blew it up. It was always restored, the fragments being collected and put together again somehow, even after the most successful demolition. When Daniel O'Connell was Lord Mayor of Dublin he had it restored and painted bronze, an extremely unpopular move in the Liberties but designed to please the powerful. I saw it in 1926 when I and my brother were driven by my grandfather's man, Mickey, in the pony-trap to see the sights of Dublin. Mickey was a Liberties man, and he repeated the Dublin saying that if the horse were to straighten its front left leg, elegantly upraised, it would prove to be eighteen inches longer than the right one. We drove on and made a U-turn around Nelson's Pillar which used to stand directly in front of the General Post Office. Mickey remarked, 'Some day we'll blow that up, and King Billy too.'

Both ends were achieved. King William was demolished in 1929 by a bomb. When the pieces were put together the head was found to be missing and its whereabouts have never been discovered. Nelson's Pillar was blown up in 1966, on the eve of the fiftieth anniversary of the declaration of the Republic. The Pillar was an ugly obstruction in a fine broad street, but some have lamented that King William was the only example of the work of Grinling Gibbons in Ireland. However, its many vicissitudes may well have left little of the original work.

In the nineteenth century the city swarmed with wretchedly poor people, many of them refugees from the country where their only food, the potato, failed year after year and left them to starve. My grandmother told me that a crowd of beggars came every day to the back door of Muckross Park, and that she often saw her father send out his own dinner-plate to them when a servant came to say that everything had been eaten up. When his wife remonstrated with him he would say, 'Give it, give it. I have enough.'

Gradually life in Dublin was becoming more comfortable for middle-class Catholics, who were said to be forgetting their duty to the common cause. The term 'Castle Catholic' dates from this time, denoting those Catholics who had so far conformed to the status quo as to visit Dublin Castle, the centre of much of the Lord Lieutenant's social and political life.

Some politically-minded Catholics, however, saw deliberate withdrawal from the centres of power as a perpetuation of their weakness. By 1860 they had given up hope of repeal of the Act of Union, but were now expecting a measure of Home Rule. They wished to fit themselves for office in case the time ever came for them to take over the affairs of the country. As a prominent Catholic who had attempted to beat the system by joining it, Daniel O'Connell had given his more conservative co-religionists courage to take a more active interest. His prison term for sedition, which undoubtedly shortened his life, probably frightened some of them, but on the whole there was a feeling of optimism about the future of Home Rule and the eventual reconciliation of old grievances.

This was the atmosphere in which my grandfather lived, writing dozens of newspaper articles on current affairs, editing and for a time owning the magazine *Hibernia*, studying law in Trinity College and in London, and travelling to and from Italy regularly to study renaissance painting. His law studies were not very serious, but it was the custom to be called to the Bar as part of a liberal education. As a well-off bachelor he developed a habit of collecting books, pictures and manuscripts, especially any that had some connection with Ireland, as for instance the manuscripts of Beethoven's Irish songs. He took a great interest in the literary revival which was taking place at this time, and in the movement for the preservation of the Irish language and of ancient

Guinness Brewery, Dublin

manuscripts. While still a student he presented a gold medal for spoken Irish which is still competed for at Trinity College, and the first recipient was the young Douglas Hyde who later founded the Gaelic League.

One of his most characteristic activities at this time concerned the research on neglected Irish manuscripts. William Kirby Sullivan had brought an Irish scholar named Brian O'Looney to Dublin to be professor of Celtic at Newman's short-lived Catholic University, of which Sullivan was registrar. Learning that O'Looney was unemployed when the Catholic University closed down, and that his work had therefore come to an end, my grandfather paid him an annual stipend to go on with transcribing Irish manuscripts, and he continued this stipend until O'Looney's death.

Professorships of Celtic had existed in the Queen's Colleges which were founded in 1848, but when the Royal University was set up these were abolished, with several others, as an economy measure. One can safely say that this type of economy was the most irritating to the Irish at all times, but the proposers always seemed either unconcerned with or unaware of the injury they were doing to the relationship between them and the people of the country.

This was still the period in which ambitious young literary people set out for London as soon as they had their first taste of success. One of these, a friend and fellow-student of my grandfather, was Oscar Wilde, who was suffering from the dilemma that later confused Synge and Yeats – whether or not he was Irish, whether or not he could live in Ireland and do full justice to his muse. Wilde and my grandfather had a long correspondence on this subject, complicated by Wilde's interest in the Catholic faith to which he was very much attracted. With his French and Italian experience, my grandfather had no fears that being a Catholic stamped one as belonging to the lower classes, but it was not so with the Wildes. Oscar was discouraged from his speculations and went off to Greece with Professor Mahaffy, who made a remarkable promise before they left that he 'would make an honest pagan' of Oscar.

My grandfather kept all of Wilde's letters, as he kept every article he received by post, but my grandmother burned them in a fit of righteousness during the sensational trial. At the same time his name was removed from the gilded board in his old school, Portora Royal School in Enniskillen, where the names of those to whom scholarships and exhibitions had been awarded were intended to shine forever. It was restored many years later and may still be seen there. It is not recorded how my grandfather responded to the destruction of the letters, if he knew about it, but he and Oscar remained friends to the end.

After Wilde's marriage my grandfather was a frequent visitor to his house in London during his time as a law student there. He also visited Lady Wilde, Oscar's mother, the widow of Sir William Wilde. She had moved to London after her husband's death, intending to further her son's career as a dramatist and poet by entertaining for him. My grandfather described her as very tall and ungainly, with large hands and feet, dressed in a voluminous tea-gown with ribbons and lace insertion, which brushed against and overturned the vases and ornaments and bric-à-brac with which her rooms were crowded. She was very kind and hospitable to anyone from Ireland and always wanted news of the nationalist movement there.

Like so many of the Victorians, Lady Wilde had kept bundles of letters, including some addressed to her husband. One day she handed these to my grandfather with the request that he read them and destroy anything scandalous. Scandal was the great crime then. He found one letter which he faithfully destroyed, but inevitably put all the rest away safely. Nearly fifty years later my mother discovered them and gave them to the National Library of Ireland. Among them were several letters in which Oscar was referred to as 'the madman' – this in correspondence with his father, surely with encouragement. Sir William and Lady Wilde were a strange and incompatible pair, she writing intensely patriotic articles and verse for the *Nation* newspaper, he a typical Victorian doctor, gifted and eccentric, both of them full of a kind of uncontrollable talent which was almost certain to result in descendants of genius. My grandfather told me once that he disliked Sir William Wilde and thought his wife deserved a better husband.

It was during this period while he was a student in London that my grandfather saw a great deal of William Butler Yeats, who was still struggling to find a supportive philosophy for his raging poetic talent. Hypnotism and 'white' magic fascinated him, but not everyone shared his enthusiasm. On one occasion he attempted to hypnotise Maud Gonne, but she refused to co-operate, understandably, since the object was to have her wake up willing to marry him. Presently she passed into a fit of hysterics. Yeats, according to my grandfather, summoned him from his lodgings nearby and implored him to take the now loudly screaming lady home. He did, but suffered agonies of embarrassment as she passed shrieking through the crowded streets, opening the cab windows as fast as he closed them so that all London could hear. He and Yeats avoided each other afterwards, though my grandfather admired him always. I remember him writing a congratulatory letter on Yeats's poem about Roger Casement, in 1936, and speaking with admiration of his involvement in Irish affairs after the setting up of the new state.

COUNT PLUNKETT, F.S.A.

From a book of contemporary caricatures

In his travels to and from Europe my grandfather often stayed for long periods in Rome and it was there in 1883 that he befriended and funded an Englishwoman who was trying to win Papal recognition for a religious nursing community. The friendship continued and some years later it was he who invited them – now fully recognised as the Little Company of Mary – to come to Ireland and found hospitals. One unlooked-for result of this altruism was that the community recommended in the right quarter that it would be fitting recognition of my grandfather's work if he were granted a Papal title. It could not have happened at a more opportune moment.

My grandfather's mother, Elizabeth Noble, had died in 1879 and his father had remarried. His stepmother was Helena Sullivan, known in the family as Aunt Helena. It was obviously time for grandfather to find a wife of his own, and he began to pay court to his cousin Josephine Cranny, the only surviving daughter of his father's partner, with whom he had fallen in love when she was fourteen. Her mother was a sharp-tongued, domineering, very religious lady who did not relish the idea of parting with a useful daughter. But the Crannys were *molto Cattolico*. Mass on Sundays had been said in their house until Donnybrook church was finished building. A Knight Commander of the Holy Sepulchre was irresistible.

Titles are never popular in Ireland and are often the subject of derision. At first my grandfather felt embarrassed at his new designation and had no wish to use it, but presently word came to him through some emissary that it was considered impolite not to wear the title once it had been conferred on him. He submitted and in time learned to live with it. I was never sure whether my grandmother liked being a countess, but so she was addressed for the rest of her life.

When they married in 1884, the wedding took place in the newly-built church at Donnybrook and there was a reception afterwards at Muckross Park. The house was then almost twenty years old and Marlborough Road, outside the gates, had just been completed. My grandmother was given about a third of it as her dowry, and my grandfather got Belgrave Road, which had belonged to his mother. Patrick Plunkett was most scrupulous in giving Elizabeth Noble's son any of the property which could have been said to be hers.

The wedding photograph shows my grandmother in a white crinoline with flounces, a white veil with a wreath of orange-blossom, and a huge bouquet with trailing stems. Her eyes are cast down to her toes and my grandfather is looking at her with his usual gentle, kindly expression, holding his top hat safely behind his back. Two of her brothers are bearded and solid-looking. They are John, the doctor and professor, and

Gerald, the architect. The third brother is clean-shaven. He was already a remittance-man in Australia and must have come home for the wedding. He had not much liking for work and had been a thorn in the flesh of his brothers for some years before his departure. There are tales of his retreating into the workhouse in revenge for his brothers' refusal to support him, and of his threat to play a barrel organ under their office windows in town. No wonder they shipped him off in the end – but he came back to Ireland from time to time as the years went on.

My grandparents set off on their honeymoon to London, then to France and Italy and finally to America, staying away a full year. They had no sooner left than Aunt Helena set out in pursuit, having realised at the last moment that Josephine had not the remotest idea of what occurred between husband and wife after the wedding. She did not confide the result of her trip to anyone, so we can only guess at the course of that conversation.

My grandmother's ignorance was not surprising. She had been educated spasmodically at home by her brothers' tutors, but it was not considered necessary to make special provision for her except in the matter of music teachers. I had the benefit of this approach when I lived with her as a small girl. She found me a first-class teacher of the 'cello who came to the house three times a week and taught me in her presence. This man, who took music so seriously, left an indelible impression on me and opened up possibilities that I might never have encountered otherwise.

This was the good side of a Victorian lady's education. The bad side for my grandmother was that she was expected to dance attendance on her mother and also to take charge of a large part of the housekeeping, supervising the cook and the maids who were often much older than herself, telling them their business and even taking a hand in their work. She told me of a recurring terror in her life, when her mother would go out for the day, leaving instructions that a room was to be 'turned out'. This meant that the heavy Indian carpet had to be taken up and lifted out into the garden, laid across the clothes-line and beaten with a wicker implement until the dust of a year fell out of it. Sideboards, sofas, chairs, tables, beds, wardrobes, dressing-tables, wash-stands, all had to be moved, polished and dusted. Pictures had to be taken down from the walls and their backs cleared of spiders' webs, their glass shined up, the picture-rail cleaned down and the pictures re-hung. A coachman or gardener was available for things that women simply could not do with their weaker muscles. Windows were washed, the floor was scrubbed, the marble fireplace and mantel likewise, the carpet and furniture replaced, all – as in *Cinderella* – before sunset when her mother came home and inspected it. One gathered that she was not always pleased.

It would have been a relief to set out even on a much less exciting journey than that honeymoon. They were not young – my grandfather was thirty-three and my grandmother twenty-seven, and he wanted to show her the whole world. I could never make out whether or not she was interested, but perhaps she was, much like Tobias Smollett, who always noted the discomforts he suffered. She had a miscarriage in Rome and was cared for by my grandfather's old friends, the Blue Nuns. Then they left from Naples for New York.

The reason for the second part of the trip, to America, was that there was a long-lost uncle of my grandmother's there and it was suggested that they could take the opportunity of their wedding journey to attempt to find him. My grandparents traced him for quite a distance and then, according to my mother, 'they lost him among the blacks in New Orleans'.

My grandmother only referred to her first American journey now and then, once to say rather sourly that the Rio Grande was not worth all the songs about it, once to tell me that when they rode on horseback across Texas before it was settled, she left her purse on the ground at the camp site and the whole party went back a day's journey and found it. In Florida they were somewhat tempted to settle down and grow oranges, but nothing came of that plan. At the same time Charles Stewart Parnell was considering growing peaches in Alabama, but he also came back to Ireland and gave his attention to politics.

The last part of the journey took them to South America. My grandmother remembered it mostly for being too hot, and that she had another miscarriage in Rio de Janeiro, attended by a 'very ignorant black maid' in the hotel, and that she was too shy to tell my grandfather what was happening to her. They travelled back to San Francisco partly by train, crossing some desert about whose location I am not clear, where my grandfather told me the driver stopped the train so that the passengers could get out and refresh themselves with wild grapefruit which grew profusely on either side of the track. While they ate, he said, they were watched by prairie-dogs which stood up on their hind legs and barked.

In San Francisco they met my grandfather's uncle, Philip Plunkett, who was one of the earliest settlers there. Another cousin was Dudley White, who according to family tradition set up the first chemist's shop in San Francisco.

In New York, my grandfather sought out the Irish political exiles, John Boyle O'Reilly, John Devoy, Jeremiah O'Donovan Rossa and others with whom he had corresponded from time to time. He also met and introduced his bride to various cousins, the sons of Patrick Plunkett's brothers, who had gone to New York in the decade between 1820 and 1830. One of them had bought a large piece of land in Astoria on Long Island, which later became the site of the New York gas-works, in which he was also concerned. He and his family became close friends of my grandfather and they corresponded with each other for many years.

After this rousing start, at the end of a year of wandering my grandparents came back to set up house in Dublin. Patrick Plunkett had bought them a house, 26 Upper Fitzwilliam Street, and furnished and decorated it for them. They had been given wedding presents of furniture made by Dublin craftsmen – I remember an enormously long oak table, extendable by many leaves, chairs to match, and a sideboard with a back of looking-glass, carved with animals and fruit and flowers. My grandfather's pictures went up on the walls – Barry's *Lear and Cordelia* and a Rubens Nativity were the most spectacular.

He resumed his interest in politics and stood for several 'lost' constituencies in Parnell's nationalist party. These were constituencies where it was important to present a candidate in an area well known to be committed to the unionist side. He admired Parnell and they liked one another. On his last visit to Dublin Parnell called to see him, but my grandfather was out, and he always regretted missing that final meeting. They were poles apart educationally – Parnell was the most unbookish of men – but their common interest in the poverty-stricken masses of the people brought them together.

Through his association with Parnell's party my grandfather became aware that the voters' list in the St. Stephen's Green area badly needed reform. It had not been brought up to date for years, and entire families who had long moved out of the district were entitled to come back and vote there – and did. Meanwhile the real inhabitants had no votes at all. He conducted the investigations and paid his own employees to do this work, rather to the chagrin of my grandmother. The cost was more than two thousand pounds, a huge sum at that time.

When their eldest child was about to be born, a nursery was set up on the top floor of the house. It consisted of two rooms, one for the daytime and the other a night nursery, which must have been more than adequate in the beginning. But even when six other children appeared, no extension to their quarters was thought to be necessary.

At noon every day my grandmother went up 'all the way', as she told me, to the nursery, and stayed a short while with the children. The two nurses did not enjoy these visits, especially since while she was there they were obliged to address the children as 'Master George' or 'Miss Geraldine', even when they were bottle-sucking infants. In the

evening, just before they went to bed, the children were brought down to the dining-room dressed in their uncomfortable best, to be inspected and to stay a short while with the parents, and to be given a little dessert from the high table. This was the way in which my grandmother had herself been brought up, and she distinctly remembered that when she was five years old her father surveyed her kindly one evening saying, 'And what is the name of this little one?' At least my grandparents could always tell their children apart. No doubt the large mortality rate among children had made the older generation loth to get attached to them, lest the effort might be wasted. Four children survived in Patrick Cranny's family, but at least the same number died.

My mother was born in 1891, the third girl and fourth child of this establishment. When she was a baby, a nurse named Biddy came and stayed for nine years. During her reign, through three more babies, everything ran smoothly. The nurseries were clean and tidy, the children's clothes were washed and starched and ironed, they had hair-ribbons and stockings and handkerchiefs, they were taken to play in Fitzwilliam Square. Biddy sang patriotic songs and played games with them, and spent her scanty free time knitting stockings for her mother in County Meath. Then, my mother said, my grandmother came back from Paris after an absence of some months and decided that Biddy was taking too much on herself, and sent her away.

The loss of Biddy was like the loss of a mother, and it created a hatred of the Victorian attitude to servants in all the children. To my grandmother it was no more than if she had given away an inconvenient dog. She told me once that servants were 'different clay'.

The centenary of the Rebellion of 1798 was celebrated with tremendous enthusiasm throughout Ireland. New ballads were written, monuments were erected in many towns and villages and there was a revival of nationalism which must have come very near sedition and was closely linked to the revival of the Irish language through the work of the Gaelic League. The founder of the Gaelic League, Douglas Hyde, was dismayed at the turn things were taking and would never contribute to the new political spirit that swept through the country. Biddy sang the ballads commemorating the Wexford contribution. She knew dozens of them, and many older ones that had always been sung by the country people:

> *At Boulavogue when the sun was setting*
> *O'er the bright May meadows of Shelmalier*
> *A rebel hand set the heather blazing*
> *And brought the neighbours from far and near.*

> *And Father Murphy from old Kilcormac*
> *Spurred o'er the rocks with a warning cry.*
> *'Arm, arm,' he said, 'for I've come to lead you,*
> *For Ireland's freedom we'll fight or die.'*

The tunes were unforgettable, and the whole effect was exciting and dramatic. Another was:

> *'Twas early, early all in the spring,*
> *The birds did whistle and sweetly sing,*
> *Changing their notes from tree to tree,*
> *And the song they sang was 'Old Ireland Free'.*

My grandmother sang to the harp Thomas Moore's lament for Sarah Curran, the pathetic fiancée of Robert Emmet who was hanged, drawn and quartered in Thomas Street in Dublin, in 1803, for fomenting a rising:

> *She is far from the land*
> *Where her young hero sleeps*
> *And lovers around her are sighing,*
> *But coldly she turns*
> *From their gaze and weeps*
> *For her heart in his grave is lying.*

In spite of this new rebel spirit, life went on pleasantly enough. The pony and trap in Fitzwilliam Street were chiefly for the use and amusement of the children. Most of them could fit in it and sometimes they would set out for Dun Laoire – then known as Kingstown – with one of the older children driving. They were often chased along by a bored tram-driver who livened up his day by ringing the tram-bell loudly and incessantly, to see if he could make the pony bolt. Another sport in Dublin then was for rude passers-by to shout comments at equipages that looked silly. My mother remembered one that was directed at very small ponies: 'Put a knot in the pony's tail or he'll jump through the collar!' One might yell after a slow, plodding horse, 'Get down and milk it!' This remark extended into my own youth, when I went to an Irish-speaking school in Earlsfort Terrace, next door to Alexandra College, the Protestant school which was then not too sympathetic to things Irish. As we toiled in on our bicycles a voice would call out from next door, in a mixture of English and execrable Irish, *'Téigh síos agus milk é!'*

It cannot have been convenient to bring up a family in Fitzwilliam Street. My grandparents were constantly renting houses in other parts of Dublin, always keeping Fitzwilliam Street as a refuge for themselves but using the rented house as a place to deposit their children, much as they often let a house while reserving one room for their overflow of books.

About this time, at six or seven years old, my mother began to realise how casual was my grandmother's housekeeping. When she came to visit the children she brought large quantities of food, but when this was used up there was no more until her next visit. My grandmother had installed some very well-bred Black Minorca hens and a cock, on the assumption that superior hens laid superior eggs. The door of the hen-house was kept locked and my grandmother had the key. However, one of the little girls found that she could get in through the hens' door, and she was able to hand out the eggs to the others. When I was a small child, this same aunt of mine bitterly recounted to me various other deceptions to which they resorted for survival.

One is constantly struck by the dislike that seems to have existed between Victorian parents and children of this class. No doubt a great deal of it was well deserved, and of course some of it came from lack of contact. Most of my grandmother's children seem to have disliked her, though they were devoted to their gentle, kindly father. He left their daily care entirely to his wife, only intervening when he could no longer fail to notice impending disaster.

Back from their travels, perhaps from Rome, on one occasion my grandfather decided that the children were not healthy. He rented a house near Enniskerry, where he made friends with Mr. Rafferty, the coroner for South Dublin. He lived at Springfield, near Kilternan, now the Dublin Sport Hotel, and was a great traveller and connoisseur of French literature and archaeology, and a collector of clocks. A year or so later, Kilternan Abbey and the village were for sale and my grandfather bought them to be near his friend. The family moved there, but kept Fitzwilliam Street, of course.

By a coincidence, 'St. Mary's Abbey at Kilternan' had been listed among the possessions of Oliver Fitzwilliam, Margaret Plunkett's son, restored to him in 1663. It was a wonderful old house, but my mother told me that there were eleven ways by which it could be entered. When the children were left alone there, without enough servants, they were petrified with fear at night. The watch-dogs would bark, increasing their terror, and the timbers of the old house creaked like a sailing ship at sea. Nevertheless, now for a few years when they were not briefly at school, they had a marvellous time. There were dogs and cats and cows and saddle horses, and a big carriage horse named Jerry from which my grandmother tried to breed a foal, until my grandfather gently pointed out to her that Jerry was not a stallion.

Another of her projects was to grow fruit for the Dublin market. Her impulsive nature and lack of formal education made it impossible for her to study exactly how to go about this and not only did her crops do badly but also in a good season she flooded the market and reduced the prices. Besides, the traders in Dublin recognised her as an easy mark, and often named their own price anyway. Somewhere in her mind there lurked the notion of the 'wonderful woman' who can do everything well, but she was never one to rise in the night and give a prey to her household and she never got over her disdain for the lower orders who could have told her exactly how to do things, if she had allowed them to. Kilternan had huge greenhouses with grapes and peaches, as well as espalier pears and apples and plums and soft fruit of all kinds, in the walled garden. An expert gardener could have done something sensible with them.

My grandmother never lost her fear of servants and never looked at them directly. One story about this aberration concerned Johnny Doherty, who was employed as a yardman at Kilternan but who preferred to spend his time playing with the children. This might have been overlooked if he had not attempted to defraud the family of goods, bought for himself on the Plunkett account at Clery's, which he said were to be sent to Harcourt Street station to be collected. The manager wrote for confirmation of the order and Johnny was found out and sacked. The children were desolate without their playmate and my grandmother went to an employment agency in Dublin to find a replacement. A day or two later the smaller children came running in, delighted, calling out that Johnny Doherty was back. My grandmother said, 'Nonsense, nonsense! Johnny Doherty was sacked for dishonesty. That is the new man!' They said, 'Excuse us, but Johnny Doherty is back, working in the yard. The horses were glad to see him.' They were proved right, and my grandmother somehow managed to blame them but her stock fell to nothing. I have never heard how she managed to get rid of Johnny the second time. She had simply failed to look at his face when she hired him.

Every morning the parents were driven in the carriage to Sandyford station to catch the train into Harcourt Street, where they took a cab to Fitzwilliam Street to spend the day there. They bought a paperback novel each at the bookstall in Sandyford to entertain themselves on the way, though the journey cannot have taken much more than half an hour. The books were later stored in the attic in Kilternan, where my mother spent many a wet day reading them until her head ached. She learned a great deal from them about how the other half lived. These novels cost sixpence each, and when the price

went up to a shilling the supply became rather smaller.

The Victorians' appetite for reading was phenomenal, as various and copious as their appetite for food. Yet they complained that their sight was not good, and my grandfather attributed his weak sight, which lasted him for ninety-six years, to the bad habit of reading in bed by moonlight as a boy.

The sixpenny novels were of course recognised as trash. My grandfather, who was writing a monumental work on Botticelli, always went on with his book-collecting. He visited one or two bookshops every day in Dublin, Greene's in Clare Street and Webb's on the quays being favourites, bringing home a small armful every time, so that Kilternan and Fitzwilliam Street were crammed with books.

The children had access to them all. For my mother, denied any regular education, this was a blessing. A few terms with the Sacred Heart nuns when she was small, leave to sit in with tutors of mathematics who came to teach the boys, and two terms at Mount Annville boarding school made up her formal education, but she found to her surprise when she entered the university that it was adequate.

Victorian ways survived in Dublin well into the twentieth century. As her daughters grew up, my grandmother adopted the plan on which she herself had been brought up. Each of them was obliged to run the household for a week in turn, with distant and unwelcome supervision from their mother. From Biddy's patriotic songs and from their father's concern for the poor and distressed, they were all ferociously democratic. More than one of them complained to me of the anger they felt at having to order rabbits for the maids while they ate roast lamb in the dining-room.

My grandmother's own contribution consisted in dusting the piano; when I lived in her house as a child she impressed on me very strongly that the care of all the musical instruments was the special concern of the lady.

My grandfather had charge of buying the wine, of which there was always plenty. In the autumn, every year, tiny sample bottles would come from Bordeaux to be tasted. Then the barrels were ordered. When they came, the wine was bottled by a man from a public house who came for a day or two to do it. At Kilternan my grandfather went to the 'Golden Ball' to ask for this service and found that the owner had a hundred dozen of good claret in his store. My grandfather bought the lot at a shilling a bottle, considered cheap even in those days, perhaps indicating that wine was not much drunk in Ireland then.

Now and then a child would be sent to school, at home or abroad. The children liked Mount Annville, when they were allowed to stay there, because the food was good and they did more or less as they pleased, and they had the added pleasure of visits from their father. Their stays there were few and far between, however. One daughter was sent for a year to a good school run by the Mesdemoiselles Marchandise in Brussels, after she had been a year at Roehampton. She spoke French well, and so a year later, at the age of sixteen, her mother dispatched her from Dublin alone to Brussels to escort a monoglot Belgian nun back to London. Arriving at the convent, well outside the city, she was informed by the portress that all was shut up for the night and that she might come back the next day. She headed back for Brussels, found a hotel, came back the next day, was given a small glass of liqueur in the parlour, was introduced to her companion and they were sent on their way. The year was 1906 when, it is sometimes imagined, young ladies were restricted in their movements.

When he was fifteen, my grandmother decided to take her eldest son, Joseph, to Paris, which then as now had a damp, cold climate in winter. There she put him in a school at Passy, where he remained for a year. He was already a delicate child, with tubercular glands in his neck and a tendency to have pleurisy, and she failed to provide him with warm clothing. At the end of the year he and the second son were sent to school at Stonyhurst in Lancashire, also with an unsuitable climate. Here their feelings of Irish nationalism were further stimulated. As in all English schools for the upper classes, they were expected to join the Officers' Training Corps for the British army and to take part in summer manoeuvres on Salisbury Plain. It was thus that they acquired their knowledge of warfare which they used to foment and partly conduct the Easter Rising of 1916.

The lease of Kilternan was short, and as the children grew up it was not renewed. A sad story and an astonishing coincidence are fixed in my mind concerning it. The nearest big house on the Dublin side was the Protestant rectory. The rector and my grandfather were friends and the children played and grew up together in warm friendship also. As time went on, the Plunkett family became involved in the Irish Republican Brotherhood and the plans for the Rising of Easter, 1916. The rector's sons, their old friends, naturally joined the British army at the outbreak of the 1914 war. A week after the Rising, my oldest uncle was court-martialled and condemned to death, as one of the signatories of the proclamation of the Republic. Of all people, his old boyhood friend was instructed to command the firing party which would execute him. He refused, and was himself court-martialled and cashiered from the army, and died not long afterwards, or so I have been told. I have never checked the end of this painful story. No doubt there were other similar incidents in those mad times.

In Phoenix Park

The house in Upper Fitzwilliam Street remained as the main family house after Kilternan Abbey had been given up. When my grandfather became the Curator of the National Museum he was thereby a first-class civil servant and he was obliged to go to a levee at Dublin Castle every year when the Viceroy came. He found this extremely distressing, as he had never been anything but a nationalist, but it had been decided that more harm than good was done to the country by educated Catholics keeping aloof from all public appointments.

To go to the Castle he had to wear a sort of uniform consisting of a black velvet embroidered jacket with cut-steel buttons, some of which are still in my possession, knee-breeches of white flannel lined with satin, white silk stockings with clocks, and patent-leather buckled shoes. As President of the Royal College of Surgeons his brother-in-law had had to wear a court suit of purple velvet. My grandfather found the whole affair rather shabby-genteel, with poor food and faulty ceremony, but my grandmother liked going to the official ball where she had to wear a dress with a train, specially ordered from London.

Every winter, the families living in and around Fitzwilliam and Merrion Squares entertained each other to dances. Each family decided on a date well in advance and the Plunketts always booked a pianist named Miss Gasparro, with her violinist, to play for the dancing. It was always the same violinist but his name has not survived. It was noticed that she kicked him on the ankle if he displeased her while he played.

Between them and their cousins in Palmerston Road, the Plunketts owned enough unbleached, figured damask linen to cover the floors of the double drawing-room for dancing. The linen was tacked on to the carpets, which were too heavy to be moved out. The guests usually numbered one hundred and fifty and even then the rooms were not overfilled. Supper was laid in the study and the dining-room, and the pine rafters sprang up and down visibly, without cracking the ornamental plasterwork of the ceiling below, when everyone leaped together during the lancers.

Most of the dances were waltzes and two-steps, the favourite waltz melody being '*O du mein lieber Abendstern*'. Galops and lancers were kept until the end, to use up the last ounce of energy of the young people of that energetic generation. They also danced the Boston, a variation of the two-step with a click of the heels between the steps. My mother told me that this was introduced by one Demetrius Salazar from Rome, who had come with an introduction from friends there, and who livened up all the dances for at least one season.

The entertainment began with a children's party in the afternoon and, after the

Grand Canal, Dublin

Bait digging at Sandymount

children had gone, dancing took over for the rest of the evening. At the Plunketts no one was invited to sing unless a guest had a particularly good voice, but my mother remembered with pain the performances of daughters of other families rendering their well-practised but poorly-executed songs to the embarrassment of all, at neighbouring houses. It made her deeply suspicious of amateur musicians all her life.

While the little dance-band had supper, an older man who was a friend of the family played the piano very willingly so long as he had a glass of whiskey beside him. The young people found it difficult to impress on my grandmother that the whiskey was essential to his performance.

Dancing finished at six in the morning and then the remains of supper were eaten. If too much was left over, my mother said calmly, a small dance was held the next day for the closest friends.

Almost all of those energetic young men went off to the war in 1914 and were very soon killed.

Part of chapter two has already appeared
under the title 'A Victorian Household'
in *Victorian Dublin* edited by Tom Kennedy
[ALBERTINE KENNEDY PUBLISHING
with THE DUBLIN ARTS FESTIVAL, 1980].

The annual Croagh Patrick pilgrimage

THREE

Biddy's ballads and their father's interest in politics and the revival of Irish ensured that the young Plunketts would take an active part in the Rebellion of 1916. In Dublin, half-clothed beggars thronged the streets. My mother remembered a woman wearing only a skirt and a tattered shawl, running after the dog-cart in which she and her uncle were driving, screaming for alms. He emptied his pockets of everything he had, but this kind of charity was a drop in the ocean. A summer spent in Llandudno in 1899 and another in Rhyl a year or two later showed that the Welsh country people had a far better time of it than the Irish. On holidays in Ventry in County Kerry the children had seen people living in beehive huts of prehistoric origin, with no chimneys, and with the pigs inside. In 1909 five of them were sent with a cousin as chaperone to Dugort in Achill, to a lodging-house run by the sister of one of the Protestant clergymen associated with the Achill Mission. This had been recommended to their mother without the detail that the people who ran it were extremely unpleasant and uncongenial and though the young people complained she would not allow them to move.

The poverty of Achill in those days was vile, with horses, pigs and calves kept in the houses and an air of unwanted evangelicalism hanging over all. The wife and children of the district inspector of the Royal Irish Constabulary were the other honoured guests and the horrors of their company were never forgotten. The lady never spoke to the young Plunketts, but she once sent a note along the table asking if one of her children could have an orange off their dish of fruit, provided by their mother each week in compensation for abandoning them in such company.

They ranged all over the island and swam from the pier, watched by an old seal on a nearby rock. They found a sod hut with lobster-fishers living in it, on the hillside. When the wind blew in a certain direction they smelt the Norwegian whaling station on Inishkee nine miles away. They saw that the land had not been drained for centuries and that the children were silent, huddled over the fires, clothed in rags, and starving. They came back from that holiday certain that their generation was charged with the task of changing the lives of the Irish people.

It was in Achill that they first learned a little Irish. Their teacher, Seán Ó Longáin, took them on the annual climb up Croagh Patrick, the steep rocky mountain on which tradition says that Saint Patrick spent Lent. Thousands of pilgrims still climb that mountain every year, in early July, and Mass is celebrated on the summit. My oldest uncle, Joseph, was then twenty-one years old and in poor health, and he collapsed after the strenuous outing. He had lived with ill-health for so long that he had decided not to allow it to limit him. At Stonyhurst he had studied philosophy and the Christian mystics and through them had reached an equilibrium which detached him from self-interest. To James Connolly, his colleague in the armed uprising of 1916, it seemed like courage. During the hostilities he remarked to someone that 'Joe Plunkett has more courage in his little finger than the rest of us put together.'

Two years before that climb on the mountain he had devised a plan for a rebellion, the one which was eventually put into operation. He had come to the conclusion that only by an armed rebellion, in the style of the Fenians, would Ireland achieve better living conditions and some measure of economic development. To this end he had studied the British army manuals which were available everywhere at the time, and had realised that the best tactician always knows what the enemy is likely to do. It was an age of small wars, the Boer War, the Russo–Japanese War, the Balkan wars. A gun was a beautiful piece of machinery, to be taken apart and put together again with precision. With his whole generation Joe accepted his place in this scheme of things, presumably knowing that no other was possible. There was nothing dreamy or withdrawn about him, though for a time after his death this was a popular view – the right hand plotting troop movements, the left turning the pages of Saint Augustine.

Above all, it was not possible for the Plunkett children to believe, as their mother appeared to do, that the poor accept their station in life and have no wish for anything better. Her indifferent provision for them meant that they knew cold and hunger at first hand, though in their case it was not necessary. The slights of the governing classes to everything Irish, the patronising attitude, the often overt implication that the Irish were necessarily inferior racially, all combined to rouse in them a resolution to twist the lion's tail once more.

The lion at the time thought he was doing rather well by Ireland. Augustine Birrell, the cheerful Chief Secretary for Ireland, wished the country well and was anxious to do his best for it, even to spending more time there than was usual. A college of the National University of Ireland had just been opened in Dublin, in a convenient position just off St. Stephen's Green, with a long stone façade behind which were placed miserable, cheaply-built halls and lecture rooms. My mother was already a student in

St. Patrick's Day parade, Dublin

Looking down the Liffey towards the Four Courts

Mass is celebrated on the summit at dawn

Pause for prayer on the scree near the summit

the medical faculty, housed in Cardinal Newman's tumbledown old medical school in Cecilia Street. The College of Science was a fine old building in Merrion Street, and my father, his doctorate of science achieved, was teaching there for a salary of ten pounds a month. He had refused to take the required oath of allegiance to the king and had no prospect of promotion.

The Land Commission was trying to clean up the Augean stable which had not been hosed out for two centuries, holding enquiries, abolishing absenteeism and re-allotting holdings of land to landless farmers. A few agricultural colleges were set up, more elegant than useful.

There was no pleasing the Irish. Almost a century before, Shelley's friend Walter Savage Landor wrote:

> *'Ireland never was contented –'*
> *Say you so? You are demented.*
> *Ireland was contented when*
> *All could wield the sword and pen,*
> *Wearing, by Saint Patrick's bounty,*
> *Emeralds large as half a county.*

In fact the colonial idea, giving the colonies the privilege of producing flocks and herds to feed the mother country, in return for patronage and benevolent supervision, was never appreciated in Ireland. The Home Rule Bills proposed from time to time were considered too limited, and suggested that the supervision was not so benevolent as it appeared to be. Still, my grandfather offered himself to John Redmond, the leader of the Irish Party, as a candidate for election but he was turned down because 'his connections were unsuitable'. Connections? My grandfather was furious. His children knew it, because when he heard that his offer was refused he said 'Pouf!' Later he realised that Redmond was thinking of his connection with Parnell who was thought to have gone much too far in his demands on behalf of the peasantry. Redmond, as it turned out, was not in a great hurry and was moving at a snail's pace towards a token Home Rule.

Throughout the country the study of Irish went on, in summer schools in remote places, in the Aran Islands where Synge had gone, and in the towns in evening classes run by the Gaelic League. Through pressures from the Society for the Preservation of the Irish Language, Irish was taught in the schools though it was illegal to use it for official purposes even if it was the only language one had. There had been a classic murder trial in Connemara in the 1890s in which two brothers were condemned to death, never having understood a word of the evidence against them and denied the services of an interpreter. This did not happen in Birrell's time, but poor western peasants were still often prosecuted for having their names on their carts in Irish.

In Donegal at the summer Irish school my uncle was remembered forty years later by an old man who told me that in spite of his ill-health he was always the most cheerful, always the one who fetched the piper and started the dancing, or who got someone to sing or tell stories of the ancient heroes when the members of the school gathered in the cottages to sit by the fire in the evenings. This chatting and story-telling was a recognised form of entertainment until very recently and was known as *áirneán*, which originally meant a spinning session. Conversation was an art to be practised and it was at these sessions that the major part of the language learning went on. I have heard long discussions between countrymen on etymology and dialect on evenings like these.

On his return to Dublin my uncle was recommended a teacher of Irish to continue the lessons at home. It was Thomas MacDonagh, another apprentice poet, and a friendship began which lasted until both were executed by firing squad in 1916.

Poetry had been a way of life for my uncle for many years. Unlike his two colleagues, MacDonagh and Pearse, he had never had proper access to the mine of Gaelic poetry which was their inspiration and model. Whether this was a great disability or not is uncertain: it meant that he used more conventional rhythms and forms, perhaps even feeling bound to them, where the other two were freer, as indeed Irish poets are to this day, to use assonance and irregular metres which correspond roughly to the strange irregular music of Ireland, as old as the country itself. Pearse's poems contain passionate statements of his patriotic ideals, as well as of the gentle, visually beautiful things that attached him so deeply to his country. MacDonagh was rooted in an exuberant life that poured itself out inexhaustibly:

> *O Beauty of Wisdom unsought*
> *That in trance to poet is taught,*
> *Uttered in secret lay,*
> *Singing the heart from earth away,*
> *Cunning the soul from care to lure.*

Joseph Plunkett's poetry was entirely personal and intellectual, still steeped in the Christian mysticism which continued to fascinate him, and in Blake, but with an individual voice and continuing development of technique. These three delighted each other, all different but all exhibiting a certainty of approaching death. My uncle's version was:

Rougher than death the road I choose
Yet shall my feet not walk astray,
Though dark, my way I shall not lose
For this is the darkest way.

.   .   .

But who shall lose all things in one,
Shut out from heaven and the pit
Shall lose the darkness and the sun
The finite and the infinite.

Pearse's equal certainty was expressed in a poem in Irish, translated by MacDonagh with the special felicity he had in all his translations:

Naked I saw thee,
O beauty of beauty,
And I blinded my eyes
For fear I should fail.

.   .   .

I have turned my face
To this road before me,
To the deed that I see
And the death I shall die.

I once asked my mother straight whether they were as certain of death as these poems suggest, and she remembered MacDonagh remarking almost casually that after the Rising they would all be dead in a week, and that he and Pearse and my uncle had made their literary wills. My uncle's included a direction to my mother to make a specific collection of his poems, which she did in the autumn of 1916, after his death.

Narrow nationalism was never the aim of these embryo revolutionaries, and it is not the aim of the main body of the Irish people today. My uncle was somewhat different from the rest of the group in that he had never been poor, but he was in complete agreement with them in their principal object, which was to get the poor of Ireland to raise their heads. After James Joyce left Dublin for the last time he wrote a classic description of the slums in *Ulysses*, and O'Casey did the same in his plays. Neither gives a strong enough account, according to my parents, who commonly saw five entire families housed in one room, one family in each corner and one in the middle. Emigration from the country was on an enormous scale, but city dwellers found it

Jim Larkin comes to rest in O'Connell Street

harder to get away. It is by a natural reaction that Dublin now has more municipal housing in proportion to its size than any other city in the world. James Connolly, the labour leader, was so enraged at the conditions under which the workers had to live that he was prepared to lead his little Citizen Army, two hundred strong, out to battle against the might of the British Empire. My uncle disagreed. In his revolutionary plannings he was determined that the next Irish rebellion would not be classed as a riot, or as he said: 'ten peasants in a field surrounded by machine guns'. If war was the game, it would be played according to international rules.

He was delighted to find that Thomas MacDonagh and Patrick Pearse had the same idea, and they were all determined that Connolly and his workers must be converted to this point of view.

There is no mistaking the admiration for Patrick Pearse among the men and women who took part in the rebellion of 1916. All of them acknowledged him as their leader. On his own statement he had been a determined separatist from the age of ten. His background among small tradesmen and small farmers gave him a first-hand experience of the daily lives of people for whom there is no escape from poverty and ignorance. When he bought a cottage in Connemara my mother and her brothers and sisters, who stayed with him there, were quite sure that it was pity for the poor and not some abstract romantic vision that forced him to spend his life in trying to bring about a revolution. This pity was only strengthened when his Connemara neighbours cheated him blatantly over repairs to the roof – my mother remembered sleeping with an open umbrella to keep the rain off her bed, in his cottage at Rosmuc.

A transport strike and subsequent lock-out of the workers in Dublin in 1913 was the final episode which clarified the motives of the revolutionaries. The Plunkett household seethed with rage and some of it touched my grandmother. She bought Sandymount Castle, which happened to be on the market, and announced that it would be a refuge for the homeless families of evicted workers. It was fortunate that no one came as she had made no provision whatever for their maintenance if they did. Because of my grandmother, James Connolly was suspicious of my uncle for a time, but they soon became firm friends.

My mother had met my father, Thomas Dillon, in the chemistry laboratories of the College of Science. She felt quite at home there and while still an undergraduate was encouraged to follow a line of research on vegetable and other dyes, and to contribute to the article on dyes in the *Encyclopaedia Britannica*. Through this work she discovered the delights of chemical research and, though she never graduated, she later became an expert on this subject, making her own dyes from lichens and various vegetable materials and experimenting with them on Connemara wool and on pottery.

My father was one of her first inspirations in this. He was the grandson of that same William Kirby Sullivan who had once been the Registrar of Newman's Catholic University and who had brought Brian O'Looney to Dublin to work on old Irish manuscripts. His background made it inevitable that he would be associated with every attempt at reform, and his introduction into the Plunkett circles drew him slowly but surely into the affairs of the impending rebellion. Family tradition inclined him to use the system rather than to attack it head on, but on this occasion he also became convinced that nothing but a violent demonstration would ever improve the condition of Ireland.

The Rising of 1916 which, as it turned out, was successful in the end, continued in the tradition of such rebellions in containing a very high proportion of well-educated people. Armed uprisings are never popular with the people on whose behalf they are undertaken, since no one can tell for some time whether things will be better or worse afterwards. But this one, especially in the country, sent a strong current of hope through people who hardly knew what it was they wanted. An old lady who was sixteen years old at the time explained it to me peripherally by saying, 'We were sick of the swaddies. They had nothing to do with us. We had seen through the propaganda and there was nothing left.' A swaddy was an English private soldier, wearing puttees.

Throughout my childhood, reminiscences and anecdotes built up in my mind some picture of how it was to be alive and present during that extraordinary period in Ireland. We were never told overtly unless we asked a specific question, but our ears were stretched to add to our own first-hand knowledge and to make a complete picture.

My grandmother, wearying of the war, went off to America early in 1915 and stayed away for most of the year. This cleared the way for some planning which could not have been undertaken if she had been around asking questions. None of them trusted her to keep quiet about their doings and they were determined that no advance information should leak out. Above all my grandmother was not to be told that my uncle also went to America in 1915, to take messages concerning the plans to John Devoy and Joseph MacGarrity who represented the Irish nationalists there. Chesterton's *The Man who was Thursday* was their example of how spies can infiltrate the ranks. My uncle pressed this book on everyone, notably on Michael Collins whose bible it became. Collins master-minded the war of independence in the six years that followed, but in January of 1916 he had just come from London to take part in the Rising and was employed by my mother to put my grandmother's account books in order.

It was in my grandmother's absence that it was decided to house the 'Liverpool Lambs' in the stables and outhouses at one of her properties in Kimmage, called Larkfield. These were the Irish who came over for the Rising, and were so christened by my second uncle, George, as a compliment to their terrifying appearance. That same uncle marched them to the tram in Kimmage on the morning of Easter Monday, 1916, and when the frightened conductor saw them clambering into his vehicle he recognised that this was an act of war. The story goes in the family that my uncle George, not noted for his sense of humour, drew himself up and said, 'We are honest men. We will pay our fare like everyone else.' And he disbursed twopence for each man.

During the First World War it was possible to travel in Europe and Joseph Plunkett therefore asked his father, then aged sixty-five, to do two errands for the Irish Volunteers. The first was to memorise a letter to Sir Roger Casement, who had been promised a consignment of arms in Germany, to write it down in Berne and then to send it to Casement through the German ambassador there. The letter named the date of the proposed Rising and requested that the arms, some German officers and a submarine should be dispatched to Tralee bay, the submarine then proceeding to Dublin. As is well known, that plan misfired. My grandfather's second errand took him to Rome, to make use of his special privilege as a Papal Count to have a private audience with Pope Benedict XV.

The reason for this latter expedition was that the English Prime Minister, Asquith, had just paid a visit to the Pope, at the end of a tour of the battlefields of France. The Irish Volunteers suspected that there had been an opportunity to discuss the position of Ireland during the conversation. If the insurrection were condemned from Rome, the chances of its obtaining a solid backing in the country would be greatly reduced. My grandfather was received by the Pope, who soon revealed that Asquith had indeed spoken of Ireland, saying that the Home Rule Bill was already on the Statute Book and that thenceforward there would be no reason for any Irishman to be disloyal. My grandfather explained the true situation, the knowledge of which had been obtained from friendly sources in Dublin Castle. Conscription in Ireland was planned and any Irish Volunteers who resisted were to be disarmed, and the disaffected arrested and deported. One imaginative general had suggested that they could be forced to the battlefields and conveniently shot for refusing to fight. Partition of Ireland was to take place, and the plantation of Ulster, of which the native Irish had been deprived three hundred years before, would then be permanently ratified. The Ulster Volunteers were to retain their arms and would defend their position. The rest of Ireland, containing the majority of the population, without arms, would have no way of redressing their wrongs. My grandfather explained that the young men and women of Ireland were not prepared to submit to these new and repressive developments and had decided to rise up against them.

The Pope was greatly moved by this information, so much so that he wept in sympathy with the young men who, as they both knew, were certain to die for their principles. He sent his blessing to the Irish Volunteers and promised to pray for them, and some time later sent a contribution of five thousand pounds, a huge sum in those days, to the White Cross fund, which had been founded to take care of the dependants of the Volunteers.

Naturally, there were some who suggested that my grandfather had never made it to Rome at all, but proof turned up many years later. In 1946, when he died, my mother, going through his immense collection of documents, was astonished to come upon his hotel bill for that week in Rome. It is now in the National Library.

The Rising of Easter Monday, 1916, was a much smaller affair than had been originally planned. An inner circle had decided to go ahead even if the German arms consignment failed to appear, but the official plan was that the project was to be abandoned unless the necessary arms arrived. When they did not, the order to rise was quite correctly countermanded by the commander-in-chief, so that the country at large did not respond. But since those who went on with it believed that they were about to be arrested anyway, they preferred action to submission. Even after so many years, uncertainties and doubts as to what really happened cause endless, fruitless argument. It was a mad, wonderful piece of foolishness. A plebiscite taken a day before would have revealed an overwhelming majority wishing to remain in the United Kingdom, but within a few months opinion had swung quite the other way.

In Dublin, Thomas MacDonagh and the lanky scholarly Éamon de Valéra commanded the Volunteers in Boland's flour mills, blocking one approach to Dublin from the port. Countess Markievicz, dressed in the uniform of the Citizen Army, led out her boys who were to act as messengers, then went with the men to occupy the College of Surgeons. Others occupied the Four Courts, Jacob's biscuit factory and the large building of the Mendicity Institute on the Liffey. Pearse, Thomas Clarke the old Fenian, James Connolly with the Citizen Army, and my uncle occupied the General Post Office with their men. From these and other points they went through the time-honoured motions of getting an armed rebellion under way, buoyed up in spite of their certainty of failure with a sense of the necessity of what they were doing.

My parents had been married the day before the Rising. Since by this time the whole Plunkett family was under observation by the authorities, two policemen from Dublin Castle were present at the marriage, which took place in the sacristy of Rathmines parish church. The parish priest had neglected to mention that, according to the rules of the Catholic church at that time, Easter Sunday was counted as part of Lent, and therefore the marriage could not be celebrated in the main body of the church, nor could there be a nuptial Mass. My mother retained a grievance on this count, and it was the only detail of her wedding, besides the fact that she wore a hat instead of a veil, which she would consent to discuss.

Next morning they set out for the Metropole Hotel, directly opposite the Post Office, where they placed themselves at a window in an upstairs room, overlooking the street. From their position they saw the Volunteers and the Citizen Army march into the Post Office. Soon after noon, the flag of the Republic went up and Pearse, accompanied by several others in Volunteer uniform, stepped into the middle of the street to read the proclamation of the Republic. At the same time, my father's friend Rory O'Connor broadcast by radio to the world that a republic had been declared in Ireland, thus ensuring that there could be no question of disposing of them all, and their Rising too, without trace.

The history of that week has been written and documented so well that there is no need to describe it again. The uncertainties of the final days and the decision to go ahead in spite of the countermanding orders had created an air of euphoria and unreality. Just returned from Rome, my grandfather went to his office in the National Museum as usual. As the time approached for the occupation of the Post Office, he hurried there and requested to be given a rifle and allowed to be one of the garrison, but to his disappointment he was told that he was too old.

My parents stayed long enough at the window to see the cavalry charge of the Sherwood Foresters, in their extraordinary uniforms, down the street from the direction of Rutland Square. Presently, they retreated at the firing from the Post Office. Then came the 17th Lancers, and after that things became more serious. My mother went to Fitzwilliam Street to soothe her furious mother and tell her what was happening, then to Belgrave Road to find her mother-in-law also bitterly angry at the doings of her new relations.

As the week went on, the battle for the centre of Dublin intensified. Barricades were erected by the British army in the region of the Post Office, and rifle and machine-gun fire raked the streets day and night. Buildings were set on fire and the glare lit up the ruined buildings. The air was filled with smoke and flying ashes. Fire brigades were not allowed to intervene. The British army officers, some with experience on the battlefields of Europe, bombarded the Post Office and the trade union building, Liberty Hall – an odd proceeding since it was not occupied. But a strong feeling existed that James Connolly and his workers were the cause of all this trouble and that they should be reduced once and for all.

When it became obvious that the next move should be surrender by the insurgents, once more the ritual was followed in accordance with the rules of war as understood in those days. Wexford, where the rebellion of 1798 had never been forgotten, had risen also, and the leaders there refused to surrender until they had personal instructions from Pearse to do so. One of their officers was escorted to Dublin to meet Pearse and to hear by word of mouth that they were to cease fighting.

The men who had signed the proclamation of the Republic were court-martialled and executed forthwith by firing squad. Some two thousand officers and men were also condemned to death and a huge grave was prepared for them at Arbour Hill Barracks. Among these were my two younger uncles, then aged about seventeen and eighteen. A press photograph shows them in their Volunteer uniforms, looking like schoolboys on a Scout outing, remarkably cheerful. By this time word had got across the Irish Sea to London that something very peculiar was going on in Dublin. John Dillon, my father's cousin who had succeeded Redmond as the leader of the Irish Party in Westminster, went to London to give an eye-witness account and to demand that some sense should be applied to the situation. Various other voices were raised, including that of George Bernard Shaw. It was decided not to execute everyone who took part in the Rising but to pack them away in various gaols, mostly in England, until the European war was over.

My uncle Joseph Plunkett was executed on May 4, at Kilmainham gaol. He was twenty-eight years old, the youngest signatory of the proclamation of the Republic. The court martial took place in Richmond Barracks, where my grandfather was also imprisoned. A party of soldiers had gone to Fitzwilliam Street and arrested him, wrecking his study and tearing his precious books, in the manner of soldiers everywhere.

For some reason which no one has ever been able to explain, when Joseph was transferred to Kilmainham his father was also taken there, but in a different vehicle. At Richmond Barracks my grandfather had spent some days in a tiny cell with thirty others, the level of urine and faeces rising daily as the slop buckets were not removed. The younger men made a pile of their coats for him to lie on. His clothes and beard and hair were in filthy condition.

Kilmainham Gaol

At Kilmainham he was conducted to a cell high above a yard. When he looked down, there was his son standing under guard looking up at him. From these positions they were able to see each other clearly, and so they remained, gazing at each other, until darkness fell. The pain for my grandfather was multiplied by the fact that my uncle was recovering from an operation for the removal of tubercular glands in his neck, and he looked as if he would collapse at any moment. Whether this encounter was meant as an act of kindness or of sadism it is now impossible to tell.

Since the previous December my uncle had been engaged to be married and, like my mother, had intended to have the wedding on Easter Sunday, the day before the Rising. However, on that day he had no time to spare for personal affairs and he wrote a note to his bride, Grace Gifford, to say that they would have to postpone their marriage until some later date. In captivity he pressed this wish on the authorities, and they complied sufficiently to allow them to be married on the night before his death. At six o'clock that evening an escort of soldiers called for Grace Gifford at her family's house in Palmerston Road, and brought her to Kilmainham. There she walked up and down alone, in a prison yard, until eight o'clock, when she was conducted to the prison chapel. The bridegroom was led in by a party of soldiers with fixed bayonets. The ceremony was conducted by candlelight, the gas having failed. Two soldiers acted as witnesses. Immediately afterwards, my uncle was taken back to his cell and his bride went to lodgings which the priest had found for her in nearby Thomas Street. Early next morning she came to the gaol once more and was allowed ten minutes with her husband in the presence of soldiers with fixed bayonets. Then he was led out to be shot.

My uncle's marriage was one of the incidents which sparked off sympathy with the insurgents. It seemed to continue in the same romantic, almost playful spirit which had imbued the whole affair. There was a core of sense in it, however. My uncle, on the Easter Sunday when the plans were concluded, had written a will in which he bequeathed any property which should have been his to the girl who was to have been his wife. A few days later he wrote her a letter, on the back of the will, and gave it to James Connolly's secretary, Winifred Carney. The General Post Office was blazing and the insurgents had moved into number 16 Moore Street and were on the point of surrender. My uncle may have hoped that Miss Carney would not be taken prisoner. She was, and long after his death, on her release at Christmas 1916, she delivered the letter:

To Miss Grace Gifford, 8 Temple Villas Palmerston Road.
6th Day of the Irish Republic, Saturday April 29th 1916. About noon.
Somewhere in Moore St.

My darling Grace,

> *This is just a little note to say I love you and to tell*
> *you that I did everything I could to arrange for us to*
> *meet and get married but that it was impossible.*
> *Except for that I have no regrets. We will meet soon.*
> *My other actions have been as right as I could see and*
> *make them, and I cannot wish them undone. You at any*
> *rate will not misjudge them.*
> *Give my love to my people and friends. Darling, darling*
> *child, I wish we were together. Love me always as I love*
> *you. For the rest all you do will please me. I told a*
> *few people that I wish you to have everything that belongs*
> *to me. This is my last wish so please do see to it.*

> *Love x x x x*
> *Joe*

Grace Gifford's sister had been married for some years to Thomas MacDonagh and had two small children. He was also executed, and my uncle had in mind the likelihood that the two women would take care of each other. My uncle was also especially anxious that Grace should be made independent, as she had very recently joined the Catholic Church in the face of some opposition from her mother.

In September of 1916 my mother carried out her brother's wish and edited a volume of his poems which ran into four editions over the next three years. One poem has lasted so long that it must be called a classic. This is the poem that grew out of his reading of St. John of the Cross:

> *I see His blood upon the rose*
> *And in the stars the glory of His eyes,*
> *His body gleams amid eternal snows,*
> *His tears fall from the skies.*

> *I see His face in every flower;*
> *The thunder and the singing of the birds*
> *Are but His voice, and carven by His power,*
> *Rocks are His written words.*

All pathways by His feet are worn,
His strong heart stirs the ever-beating sea,
His crown of thorns is twined in every thorn,
His cross is every tree.

A day or two after their brother's execution, my mother and her older sister were allowed to visit their parents in prison and to bring them some clean clothes. My grandmother, greatly to her annoyance, had been arrested on general principles, and she wanted nothing except to get out. Her lack of interest in politics and revolutions had a somewhat protective effect and she could not quite grasp the extent of the disaster that had enveloped her family. My grandfather, though heart-broken at the loss of his eldest son, felt that the object had been achieved and that this would become plainer as time went on. He was still unwashed and unkempt, but he had been moved to a new cell and it was not so crowded.

Within a few days, his living conditions changed dramatically. He was given a single cell and washing facilities. When my mother visited him he looked almost his old elegant self. Every day, he said, an excellent dinner was served to him by a soldier of the Black Watch – a number of dishes, well-cooked, on a tray. He had no idea who was responsible and the soldier would say nothing. This had continued for a week or so when one day, as the soldier with the tray appeared, so did the cook, in full regimentals, medals, tartan kilt and all. He asked anxiously whether everything was to the Count's satisfaction. My grandfather replied that the food was excellent and took the opportunity of asking who was providing it. The cook replied mysteriously; 'The Colonel says: "Remember!"'

Then he saluted grandly and marched away.

All was now clear. Some years before, my grandfather had come upon a document in French relating to the cause of the Stuart kings in the eighteenth century. He had translated it and sent it to a Scottish society which was dedicated to restoring the Stuart dynasty. Colonel Dewar of the Black Watch regiment then in Dublin was a pillar of that society. 'Remember!' was the password of Jacobites everywhere.

Within a few weeks my grandfather was informed that he and my grandmother were to be deported to any English city they named. Their youngest daughter might go with them. My grandfather chose Oxford, so that he could read in the Bodleian Library, but he found when he got there that his old acquaintances would not guarantee him as a suitable reader. In Dublin various learned societies began to strike his name off their books, including the Royal Dublin Society and the Royal Society of Antiquaries, in whose rooms a portrait of him now hangs.

Early in 1917 he was allowed to return to Ireland when he pointed out that he was a candidate in the North Roscommon by-election. His opponent was a member of the Irish Party whose leader was John Dillon. My grandfather told me that as he campaigned, the country roads were deep in snow. Miles outside the villages men had cleared the way for his car and several times he was deeply moved to see a line of them, with their shovels, standing on the piled snow, calling out as he passed, "Up, Plunkett!" He was elected by 3,022 votes to 1,708, and was the first Sinn Féin deputy to be elected to Parliament. Some months later he was back in prison again, this time for making a speech about the treatment of the Irish prisoners in England.

The old men and women who took part in that war of independence so long ago still have to be reassured from time to time that their instincts led them aright, and that subsequent generations are grateful to them. They are commemorated in bronze by Oliver Sheppard's figure of Cúchulainn, the mythical Irish hero, in the General Post Office in Dublin. The story goes that Cúchulainn, mortally wounded and the last man left alive on the battlefield, had tied himself upright to a pillar stone, and had so terrified his enemies that none dared approach him until the carrion crows alighted on his shoulders to devour him.

Thomas MacDonagh's son, the poet Donagh MacDonagh, wrote of the veterans thus:

> *And with their youth has shrunk their singular mystery*
> *Which for one week set them in the pulse of the age,*
> *Their spring adventure petrified in history,*
> *A line on a page,*
> *Betrayed into the hands of students who question*
> *Oppressed and oppressor's rage.*

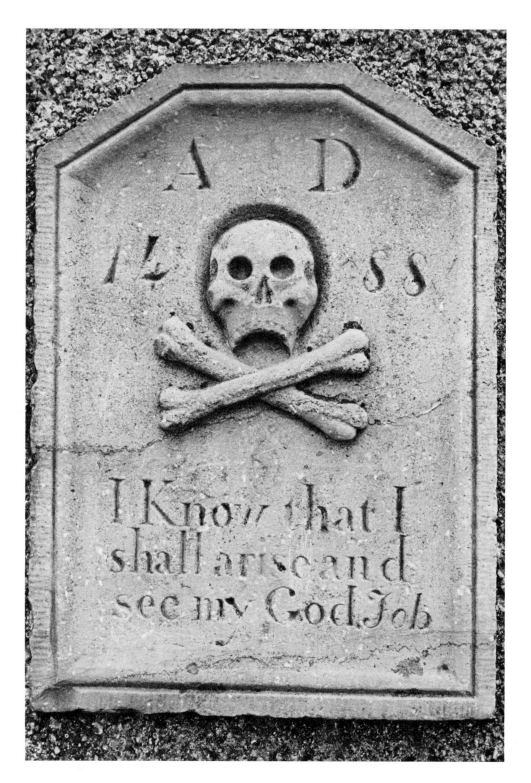

A Galway wall tablet

FOUR

♣

So I was born, in Galway, in 1920, into a world of ghosts. I was the third child of the family, my senses sharpened at a very early age to understand the things that happened to us. We lived in a state of permanent terror. Violence was all around us. The Black and Tans, the auxiliary police brought over to quell Ireland for good and all, were riding high, promised full support for their unspeakable actions, out of control even by their own officers. The army was somewhat better, but my earliest memory dates from about my first birthday, March 1921, when a party of soldiers broke into the house, upset the furniture, threw the books down from the shelves, lifted the floor-boards in their search for hidden guns, and finished by taking my mother away with them on their lorry, surrounded by fixed bayonets. It was their custom to drive through the town displaying their victim, who was put to stand where he or she could be clearly seen, so as to terrify the townspeople. It was largely successful.

My father was on the run, a familiar expression to me as a child, meaning that he had left home and gone into hiding in fear of being murdered. My older sister, then four years old, knew just what was afoot because on another occasion, not long before, she had been compelled by a party of Black and Tans to lead them out into the garden where my mother was, so that they could kill her. My mother argued them out of their intention then, saying that it would be objected to in England if they were to shoot down a young woman in the presence of her child. But now they had gone off with our mother, and my sister understood that we would never see her again.

We had one young maid-servant named Peggy, and we were left absolutely to her inexperienced care. My older sister remembered her with loathing but the strongest impression I retain of that period is a visual image of two soldiers in wide caps and puttees of dark khaki, which I never saw in my conscious life. One is standing, the other kneeling while he uproots the floor-boards of an upstairs room with a shiny knife – his bayonet – attached to the barrel of his gun.

We had moved to that house because it was in a curved terrace and could not be surrounded. The curve meant that it was not easy to identify which garden belonged to our house. Many such moves had been made since the family had come to Galway,

Dangan House, County Galway

where my father had been elected professor of chemistry at the university, the old Queen's College. The election took place while he was in Gloucester gaol, where he had been interned without trial for a year. His companions included Arthur Griffith, later Prime Minister of the Irish Free State, Robert Brennan of Wexford who was later the Irish Ambassador to Washington, and Michael Hayes, later a member of the Irish Government and professor of Irish language and literature at the National University in Dublin. My father had been taken prisoner while on a visit home, though he knew that he and all the Irish members of Parliament were to be arrested. My second sister was within a few weeks of being born, and he took a chance that failed.

My mother remained for three months in Galway gaol, loudly demanding to have me with her as the tinkers were allowed to do. Some kind soul finally asked a question about me in the House of Commons. She was released and I lost my only chance of being able to boast that I had been imprisoned for my country.

Fear remained, long after the war finished and we went to live in the country, but now it was confined to the night-time. Now there were deep silences, broken suddenly by the corncrake with its curious double rattling note which came distantly through the open window from the meadow beside the house when I lay in bed in broad daylight on summer evenings. This was Dangan House, about three miles north of Galway. It was a plain two-storeyed manor house, perhaps a hundred years old, with shallow steps leading to a wide front door. Though the Black and Tans were gone I knew it could be surrounded – that was the first lesson I had learned. As the evening darkened, instead of the tall yew-tree against which my mother had planted a rambler rose, there was a hidden mass of evil which might at any moment break loose and overwhelm us all. Instead of the quiet Corrib river at the end of a long sloping field there was a dangerous artery which might be used to reach us, as the Norsemen used the rivers in ancient times when they came to sack the monasteries. The thick stems of the wistaria that grew against the house wall could be used as a ladder to climb in at the upstairs windows. Mr. Reddington's ghost, which travelled in a coach and four along our avenue in the dead of night was not half so threatening as these realities. It would be foolish to put one's trust in parents who might be dragged away or go on the run at any moment.

The sight of a uniform terrified me. At Independence, the Civic Guards were established – they were not called police, since the very word had a bad odour. They were unarmed, and wore a dark-blue uniform with silver buttons, and a cap with a silver badge. In my nightmares, ranks of these beset our house, armed with rifles from which bayonets protruded. In the big cobbled yard, peaceful hens pecked among the weeds, but a fox broke in and slew several of them. After that, invisible foxes on soundless feet pursued me through every dark corridor and up every flght of unfamiliar stairs, even in the daytime.

The nurse, Charlotte, in whose room I slept, complained that I woke in the night and was only soothed when she sang for me. It was true that I loved her singing. My mother, by then with four children to think of, undertook to cure me of the habit, and did, in her forthright way. She took me to sleep in her room, to my great pleasure. But when the horrors of the night came upon me and I awoke, screaming for help, my mother seized me and put me outside the bedroom door, closing it firmly against me. In vain I stretched upward in the pitch darkness, trying to turn the huge china knob. I battered on the door while my enemies crept silently closer and closer, the foxes leading, the Black and Tans surrounding, soft, rubbery, unnamable bodies pressing closer and closer, until I had no more breath. Then I was readmitted to the room, where I continued to spend my nights until it was certain that the cure was complete. It was. For many years I awoke an hour or so after midnight, at the mercy of these demons, but now I knew that they were mine and that no one in the whole world could deliver me from them. Though I shivered with the abomination of it I knew it was essential to keep silence. My sisters had their demons too, and so, I gradually learned, had a great many of the people of Ireland. I can never live in the country now, because of those nights.

The days were wonderful in that beautiful place. A stream with kingfishers ran just beyond the gravel sweep before the door. On windy days the song of the pines made heavenly music. Distant dogs barked and were answered by ours. My father had preceded the family to Dangan and was expected to have produced some kind of order before the rest of us arrived. This plan included the buying of a cow. He and his houseman, Andy Hession, went to the fair together and between them managed to buy the least prepossessing beast on offer. They had her driven back to Dangan and tested for tuberculosis, and she was found to be a regular mine, a veterinarian's dream of the disease. My father arranged at once to have her slaughtered, and he was entitled to compensation of four pounds from the Galway County Council. His gardener, Batty, looked at him with contempt when he was instructed to take the cow back and turn her in as a dead loss. No one did that, he said. Far better to take her back to the fair and sell her to someone who would not be so particular about her health. After all, she was only a cow.

My father's second excursion into farming occurred the very next week. Again he went to the fair, again accompanied by Andy Hession, and again – as if they were acting

out a Grimm's fairy tale – they bought the oldest, most decrepit animal there, this time a pony. It stood upright on four legs and was attached to a trap, but my mother remarked bitterly that it was the trap rather than the pony's legs that kept it so. Somehow it tottered back to Dangan, with Andy driving, and was unharnessed in the stable yard. It stood silently while the trap was put away in the coach-house, then Batty led it out to the nearby paddock. It walked slowly into the middle of the paddock, through the lush spring grass, uttered a small cry and dropped dead.

When my mother arrived she briskly bought a small, shiny, black Kerry cow, but for the use of babies who had to survive on milk alone she also bought a goat and its mate. Goats, it was said, never contracted tuberculosis, which with typhoid was the main slayer of children and adults in Ireland then and for many years afterwards. They were strange little beasts, even their kids having scant charm for me. Their slanting yellow eyes had a gleam of mockery in them. They were just big enough to knock a child down, and they seemed to delight in doing this. Moreover, they ranged freely about the paddock, seeming to prefer the weedier corners where dock and fennel and cow parsley grew, and these they guzzled at a rate that was gratifying to our parents but not to us who had to drink their milk. It had a wild, strange tang and added something still more unsavoury to the flavour of goats, for me. The country people equated them somewhat with the evil eye, their curved horns no doubt helping out the comparison with devilish doings. To this day in Ireland one may see goats grazing with cattle and horses, not only to keep off evil but because they eat the noxious weeds that might poison the other animals.

My mother also bought a donkey, with a tiny trap, and a saddle and bridle for anyone intrepid enough to ride her. My sister did, until one day they encountered an amorous male which disturbed our donkey so much that my sister fell off. A foal ensued, the most endearing small animal in the world until his hooves had learned how to place a kick. His mother was rather old for the experience and she moved even more slowly afterwards. In fact she must have had the world's record for the slowness of her journey to Galway, in spite of yell and blow, when she took us shopping.

When the animals had been established, my mother applied herself to the garden. It had been well kept by the previous owner, perhaps with the help of Batty who was our permanent gardener now. It was a typical Irish walled garden, laid out when labour cost fourpence a day, completely surrounded by a twelve-foot wall of stone against which grew peaches and pears and apples and plums. Box hedges divided it into squares and rectangles, where all kinds of vegetables and fruit trees grew. In one part a hedge of tiny roses, pink and white, were exactly the right height for a four-year-old eye to peer into them.

From her home experience my mother knew how to take care of a house and garden of this kind. Bowls of hyacinths, vases of daffodils and tulips filled the house in spring. She took a huge, deep, Victorian soup-plate and filled it with water, then sailed a tulip-leaf on it as Thumbelina's boat. She cut miniature furniture out of the shiny horse-chestnuts that fell from the big tree at the top of the lawn. She made Thumbelina's bed, of half a walnut-shell. With her beautiful pale-gold hair piled high on her head she spent long days picking raspberries and currants which she made into jam in the flagged kitchen. She kept a weakly kid in a cardboard box by the range until it got up and walked out one day, bleating cheerfully. She set up a dairy, with glazed brown crocks in which the milk was left to allow the cream to rise to the top, when she made butter with a hand-churn. Her yeast bread filled the house with a clean fragrance. At Christmas she brought home rolls of crêpe paper and fine copper wire and made strings of paper tulips and daffodils and roses to hang from corner to corner of the drawing-room. She blew the inside out of eggs and painted the shells with gold paint or little coloured flowers to hang on the Christmas tree which Batty brought in from the grove in the paddock, and which reached quite to the ceiling. And at Christmas, too, she followed the country custom of lighting a long, thick, red candle and placing it in the drawing-room window, so that the mother of God, wandering in search of a place to give birth to her child, might know that here was a house with a welcome for her.

In her remaining free time she took plywood and a fretsaw and cut out figures of dancing women, very fat, composed entirely of circles. These she painted with faces and black shiny hair, long bright dresses and aprons with borders of tiny dots. Then she attached a calendar to the toes of each and sent them off to her friends in Dublin by the post.

And she sang. Both she and Charlotte, our nurse, had a large repertoire of songs, Charlotte's tending to be more bloodthirsty and vindictive:

> *Lord Waterford is dead, says the Shan Van Vocht,*
> *With the divil at his head, says the Shan Van Vocht.*
> *Lord Waterford is dead with the divil at his head,*
> *And hell it is his bed, says the Shan Van Vocht.*

The Shan Van Vocht – correctly *Sean Bhean Bhocht*, the poor old woman – was one of the secret names given to Ireland in the bad old times. Charlotte also sang 'The Peeler and

A country post office, County Carlow

the Goat', a derisive song about an encounter between a goat and a policeman in Tipperary which so enraged the Royal Irish Constabulary in the last century that they were able to get a boy sentenced to six months in gaol for the offence of whistling the tune.

My mother's music was altogether more gentle. She sang the songs of Thomas Moore, and George Petrie's translation from the Irish – his only effort in this direction, unfortunately – 'The Snowy-breasted Pearl':

> There's a colleen fair as May,
> For a year and for a day
> I have sought in every way her love to gain.
> There's no turn of hand or eye
> Fond youths with maidens try,
> But I've tried with ceaseless sigh and tried in vain.

Another favourite of hers was Yeats's 'Salley Gardens':

> Down by the salley gardens my love and I did meet;
> She passed the salley gardens with little snow-white feet.
> She bade me take love easy as the leaf grows on the tree;
> But I being young and foolish with her would not agree.

And she sang Padraic Colum's ballad 'She Moved through the Fair':

> My young love said to me: 'My mother won't mind,
> And my father won't slight you for your lack of kind.'
> Then she stepped away from me and this she did say:
> 'It will not be long, love, till our wedding day.'
> She stepped away from me and she moved through the fair
> And fondly I watched her move here and move there,
> And then she went homeward with one star awake
> As the swan in the evening moves over the lake.

Sometimes my mother sang the old patriotic ballads, though I think she found them too disturbing. One cheerful marching song of hers, from the opposing political tradition, celebrated the exploits of the militia of County Down, in Ulster:

> I belong to a famous regiment whose deeds are often told,
> For on the field of battle they were always brave and bold.

82

It then went into detail:

> *When Kruger heard the Regiment was landed in Capetown,*
> *'De Wet,' says he, 'we're bet,' says he, 'they've sent for the South Down.'*
> *'If that be so,' says Kruger, 'then we'd best give up the Rand –*
> *Them South Down Militia is the terror of the land.'*
> *When we went up to Aldershot in August '82,*
> *The Queen herself and the Duke were there all waiting for review.*
> *'Och, bloody war,' the Queen remarked and she waved her lily hand.*
> *'Ara, hold your whisht,' said Wolsey, 'them's the terror of the land.'*

The chorus went:

> *You may talk about your Scots Guards, Queen's Guards and a',*
> *You may talk about your Kilties and your Bonny Forty-twa,*
> *Or any other regiment under the Queen's command –*
> *The South Down Militia is the terror of the land.*

My father and the other prisoners had learned Irish in gaol, as it seems the Irish always do, and his contribution to the family concerts were in that language. Unfortunately he had no ear for music, though he loved it, and his rendering of *'Fáinne Geal an Lae'* – 'The Dawning of the Day' – was heart-rending in its inadequacy. He had other skills, however, one being his telling of stories in Irish, notably that of Munacher and Manacher who went out one day to pick raspberries, but as fast as Munacher picked them, Manacher ate them up. It was a long complicated story, collected by Douglas Hyde from a story-teller in his own area near Frenchpark in Roscommon, and my father read it with dramatic effects. I still possess the manuscript, embellished with two little drawings, one of Munacher and one of Manacher.

After his return from gaol, which was before I was born, my father never spoke English to his children again. Thus we grew up using both languages with ease. Though my mother spoke excellent French, she never mastered the sounds of Irish, which are somewhat akin to those of Russian in having broad liquid consonants and to German in their gutturals. Galway and its hinterland was then largely Irish-speaking and it was a blessing to have that door opened so easily for us.

To reach the river Corrib from Dangan House, it was only necessary to traverse a long sloping field and cross the railway line by means of two short ladders made of railway sleepers. Trains came only once or twice a day, but we darted across in fear of

Menlo Castle, across the Corrib

them. A far worse hazard was the mass of horseflies that infested the big field. These were not ordinary flies, to be frightened off with a casual sweep of the hand. They gripped, and held on until they had to be removed by force, leaving a spot of blood where their wicked little teeth had sunk in.

It was worth it, once we reached the river. There our boat was drawn up on the gravelly shore, and the oars were hidden in a tall thorn-bush nearby. The boat was eased into the water, rustling the dead rushes that lay like a mat on the water's edge, then the oars began their dipping song that sent the water lapping fast and secretly against the varnished hull. Our greatest delight was to cross the river and land at the little stone harbour of Menlo Castle, whose tall ruined chimneys were visible from the upper windows of our house. It had been a Blake castle, probably with plenty of Dillon ancestry too, and it had been inhabited until about ten years before, when it burned out accidentally. The last owner was Sir Valentine Blake, and his eldest daughter Ellen, who was an invalid, perished in the fire. A servant girl also failed to escape. Jackdaws owned it now. They had nested in the bedroom fireplaces, laying their big awkward twig nests neatly into this heaven-sent space.

On other days we rowed upriver towards Menlo village, in the direction of the lake, which stretches for thirty miles northward and is peppered with islands. One of these is Inchigoill, close to Cong, and contains a tiny cell in which St. Patrick is said to have spent some time. This was too far from us to be visited, but at present one may set out from Galway and make a tour of the lake and its islands, taking in Annaghdown with its ruined monastery on the lake shore also.

At Annaghdown a newly-erected monument commemorates the deaths by drowning of nineteen young people, from a party of thirty-one which embarked in a leaky boat to go to a fair in Galway in 1828. Tradition has it that the boat was made of tarred canvas, like the currachs on the seacoast, and that sheep which were being transported to the fair penetrated the canvas with their sharp feet. But recently some young people skin-diving found the bones of a large wooden boat on the lake-bottom at the site of the tragedy, and it is thought that this is the boat in question.

The affair is well remembered for the good reason that it was the subject of a long poem, which could also be sung, by the wandering poet Antoine Ó Raiftire, or Antony Raftery:

> *Má fhághaimse sláinte, is fada 'bhéas tráchtadh*
> *Ar an méid do báthadh as Anach Chuan –*
> If my health holds out I'll be long in telling
> Of the many drowned in Annaghdown –

It is not a great poem, but it survives today as a song, and helps to keep alive the memory of its author who was probably the last of the wandering poets of Ireland.

Raftery kept the old tradition that he was to be received with honour and given a good place at the fire and plenty to eat, 'the newest of food and the oldest of drink', and that he could stay as long as he liked and be rewarded with a saleable animal, preferably a horse which he might wish to ride to his next resting-place. I'm sure he was never given a horse.

The tradition stretches back into antiquity, as is testified by a satiric quatrain in Old Irish on the subject of a mean host who did not reward the poet sufficiently:

> *Ro-cúala*
> *Ní tabair eochu ar dúana:*
> *Do-beir a n-í as dúthaig dó,*
> *Bó.*

This has been delightfully translated by Vivian Mercier, keeping the style and spirit of the original:

> *I know him.*
> *He'll give no horse for a poem.*
> *He'll give you what his kind allows,*
> *Cows.*

The wandering poets were credited with occult powers, to the extent that they could cause death by satire. This ensured them a welcome, but Raftery's reputation was more likely to work against him. He was said to have the unwitting power of evil, so that if he praised a girl in song she would die. Names and dates are given for the occurrences. To the outlanders he must have looked like an aggressive beggar, but to the western people he was a symbol that the old way of life had not yet quite died.

In a sense his mantle fell on another writer in Irish, Pádraic Ó Conaire. He was a descendant of a long line of displaced landowners, the ramifications of whose family included the O'Malleys, the Joyces and the Conroys. When the O' fflaherties of Aughanure surrendered to Queen Elizabeth after her Irish campaign, they gave up their castles and territory and their fleet of ships on the Corrib, and then had them granted back in return for a promise of fealty. The Joyces and O'Malleys and Conroys were represented by their queen, Grace O'Malley of Mayo. She was received in London on equal terms by Queen Elizabeth, but her subjects and family did less well than the

O' fflaherties. Gradually they were reduced financially, though they lost none of their pride or their original temperament. These survived notably in Pádraic Ó Conaire, who spent many years in the Civil Service in London, then scorned the bourgeois life and set off with a donkey and cart to travel the roads of Ireland and write his classic Chekovian short stories in the Irish language.

Cecil Woodham-Smith notes in *The Great Hunger* that in the west of Ireland one is often struck by the grand manner with which a penniless countryman invites you into his three-room cottage and engages in polite conversation to put you at your ease. The only explanation, she says, is in the fact that these people are the descendants of the displaced landowners, who still carry with them a racial memory of their former greatness. Once in Cleveland, Ohio, at a television station I was greeted genially in Irish by a camera-man named Fitzmaurice, all of whose forebears had emigrated from Connemara. His Irish was limited to the greeting, but when I asked him if he knew how his family had come to Connemara in the first place, he replied that they were driven there by Cromwell's army, from their lands in Tipperary, in 1649.

Pádraic Ó Conaire slipped easily into the writer's role, which still obtains in Ireland, of the person outside society, the free impartial observer, the intellectual, who may or may not have occult powers but who is to be treated with caution in any case. A delightful little limestone statue of him sits in Eyre Square in Galway, much loved by the people of the town but now unfortunately surrounded with county engineers' concrete. It is a splendid portrait, and living versions of it in the form of his many cousins may be seen to this day throughout Connemara – the large head set at a thoughtful angle, the high intellectual forehead, and the lips pursed in concentration. The sculptor was Albert Power, who fully appreciated that his subject was another artist. Ó Conaire would have approved of the special position accorded at present to all artists in Ireland, where their earnings are untaxed, as a mark of respect.

Deprived as she had been of formal education, my mother was fiercely in favour of school. One did not wait until one was old enough to make the journey there before learning to read, however. Anyone who could not read well by the age of four was looked on with a certain amount of impatience. Following a bad scald with bath-water I had had cysts in my eyes, thought to have been brought on by shock, and these were removed by surgery. I remember lying on a round mahogany drawing-room table for the operation (which I was considered too small to understand) then being anaesthetised, probably by my mother who had not been a medical student for nothing, and being bandaged and blind for some time afterwards. It was interesting rather than

frightening – the anaesthetic was so unpleasant that all the other experiences seemed much lighter by comparison.

The loss of time involved in this meant that I could not read until I was almost five years old, which put me in the doubtful class indeed as to intelligence. Then one great day I took down Hans Andersen's *Fairy Tales* with the illustrations by Harry Clarke, and laid it on the floor by the bookcase in my father's study, where all such precious things were kept, and I read 'The Tinder Box' from beginning to end. It was such a momentous occasion that I remember the patterns of sunlight on the Indian carpet, and how the flight of white cranes on the long black curtains seemed a fitting background. I did not announce my triumph, of course. The third member of any family does ill to boast, but when I finally accompanied the others to school I found that it was useful to be able to read the books provided without having to depend on outside information.

The school was about two miles from the gates of Dangan – three if one counted the avenue as well. There was a short cut across our paddock, and then through a neighbouring field which belonged to the next big house, but this route took one rather close to the guard dog, named Ishmael. Ishmael was a large blond dog with a loud threatening bark. We were terrified of him, though I never came close enough to see his facial expression, which may have been benign enough. With a name like that, perhaps he was lonely.

So it was usually the long avenue and the long road, which seemed very long indeed in winter. Sometimes Charlotte drove us to school in the trap, but more usually we set out on foot, arriving more or less at the expected hour. I remember one occasion when we delayed a long time to address a snail that we had seen in the thick grass by the side of the road:

> *Snail, snail, put out your horns –*
> *Your father and mother are dead,*
> *And if you don't I'll break your head.*

My sisters had been informed that this would induce the snail to put out his horns if only to take a look at us, but I never remember that it worked.

The school was a miserable two-roomed building, with a tiny porch in which the children were expected to hang their coats, if they had any. There was no sanitation; the lavatories were at the top of the field in which the school stood, and were euphemistically named 'dry' lavatories. The stench was unbelievable. It was no one's business to clean them nor indeed to clean the school. The older girls were expected to do this, sprinkling the dregs of the teacher's tea-pot on the board floor to keep down the dust and then brushing the rooms out as best they could.

Heating was provided by open fireplaces, with the teacher's desk and chair placed close beside them. Everything was in the process of change but it was several years before improvements were possible in this region. The fuel used was turf, and at one time each child was expected to come to school every week bearing a penny and a sod of turf. The penny was probably a relic of hedge-school days and had long been dropped, but a few sods of turf were always welcome. The compliment to a notable scholar: 'The penny and the sod of turf were not wasted on him' survives from this custom, and is a good sample of a certain kind of Irish joke, meant to reduce rather than to commend.

Three teachers taught in the school, two women and a man. The man I regarded as a savage, who belaboured the boys and girls with ash-plants which he cut from a tree in the neighbouring churchyard. He had charge of the upper half of the school, and screams of pain came from his department at regular intervals. It was well to be safe in the junior room, where the teacher of the smallest children was Mamó. Everyone called her this – it is the Irish equivalent of 'granny', and as she was dressed like the grandmothers of most of the children, it was a compliment to include her with them. She wore a long red flannel skirt with a checked blouse, and a shawl over her shoulders which was crossed on the breast and tied securely at the back.

We loved Mamó. She must have been a monitor under the old system, a clever child who stayed on at the school as an apprentice teacher, always on a miserable wage but with no rights since she had had no special training. She taught us to write between the blue lines, a whole page of *a* in English, then a whole page of *a* in Irish, and so on through the alphabet. She had a series of pictures tacked to the walls with a story in Irish about a foolish man who lit his pipe with great care, then hurled the pipe into the river and put the match in his mouth. She taught us to spell in two languages, singing the names of the letters first, like a cantor, then having us join in, repeating the sounds over and over until they were part of our anatomy. In the same way we rhythmically sang out addition and subtraction and multiplication tables.

She taught us songs, first singing the verse herself and having us join in the chorus, then repeating the whole until we knew it thoroughly. Some of the songs were in English, some in Irish. One in English was a bitter old anti-recruiting song with a rousing chorus:

> *'Mrs. MacGrath,' the sergeant said,*
> *'I will make a soldier of your son Ted,*
> *With a scarlet coat and a big slouch hat —*
> *Now, Mrs. MacGrath, wouldn't you like that?'*

And we sang the chorus:

> *With a too-rye-ah,*
> *Fol the diddle da,*
> *Too-rye-oo-rye-oo-rye ah!*

The mother waits for a dozen long years or more for her son to come home, but

> *Teddy landed without any legs,*
> *And in their places were two wooden pegs.*
> *'Teddy, my boy, is it true? Is it true?*
> *Och, Teddy my darling, sure that's not you?'*
> *With a too-rye-ah,*
> *Fol-the-diddle da,*
> *Too-rye-oo-rye-oo-rye ah!*

And she finishes in rage:

> *'Now mighty war I will proclaim*
> *On the kings of England, France and Spain.*
> *I will make them rue the day*
> *They shot my Teddy's legs away.'*

On the surface the children were meek and silent, but they were not really at home in the English language. Though they were safe for the moment, the shouts from the other room must have filled their timid hearts with terror. Mamó's way was to reward the good with a highly-coloured boiled sweet from the can that stood always on the shelf, and to punish the wicked by hurling a small toy rabbit in their general direction. Then the victim had the pleasure of hugging the rabbit for a moment before returning it to the desk.

We soon progressed to little reading-books, intended for English schools, with moral stories about the dangers of walking alone in the park, or indulging in fine silk clothes, or drinking so much that one's family suffered. In this last story, the poor wife is putting on her bonnet and shawl to go to the Saturday-night market for food when her reformed husband hands her two pounds instead of the one to which she was accustomed. From the point of view of the children in that school, a pound was untold wealth, and as for the market, she might as well have been going to the casbah.

In time we found out that we knew not two but three languages. In choosing this school for our early education our parents had come in for some criticism. We would be consorting with dirty, sickly children who might infect us with diseases, our accents would suffer, we would develop a habit of indiscriminate friendships. All of these arguments were true, but our parents had such faith in the new world they and their friends had created that they were prepared to take the risk on our behalf. In the event, we spoke Irish to our father, good Victorian Dublin English to our mother and her friends, and what would have been called dialect in any other language to our acquaintances at school. An example was that when the kettle boiled for Mamó's cup of tea half-way through the morning we all called out, 'The kittle's bilin', Ma'am.'

We lived too far away to make friends at school, in any case, but we had no difficulty in discerning that clean clothes and a well-scrubbed face can cover a repulsive nature, and that the gentlest and pleasantest of our companions were often the dirtiest.

My father in the meantime set to work on the chemical department of the university. The Queen's Colleges had been opened in Cork and Galway in the middle of the last century, during the decade when famine and emigration reduced the population by twenty per cent. The buildings were cut stone, the Galway one somewhat smaller than that at Cork, but elegant in its neo-Gothic way. My father's department consisted of two largish rooms with about eight benches and a dozen bunsen burners and little else. Most of the students were in the medical faculty, and had not much use for chemistry. It was his business to convert this situation into something closer to what he had left behind in the College of Science and to what he knew from visits to English and European universities, but in the early years he and all his serious colleagues were hampered by lack of money. The Civil War which had followed on the Treaty had cost the country so much that for a time all works came to a standstill. My father's temperament became fixed at that time into a fanatical desire to build up the country that Pearse had envisaged, where everyone would have an opportunity of education, where the education offered would be suitable to the country and the people, and where self-confidence would replace the dispirited attitudes which stultified all progress. It was about that time that he began to dream of an industrialised Ireland, not on the model of England in the last century, but one in which the resources of the country would be mainly used. Pharmaceuticals could be manufactured anywhere, for instance, especially with an intelligent work-force. No one need be rich, but there should be interesting, suitable work for everyone that wanted it. The idea that an Irishman was only fit to carry a sack on his back would disappear. Small local factories would support their own community. To this end, he and a partner set up a soap factory in the stableyard at Dangan.

In no time at all he learned a lesson. Factories need capital and management as well as technical skill. The partnership failed for various reasons and my father was cured forever of trying to enter the world of business. The lesson took such good effect that in later life he would not even try to patent his discoveries, some of which were and are used in industry at great profit to other people. Knowledge belongs to the whole world, he said, and anyone who sees its possibilities may set to work on it. Somewhere, somehow, the benefit will accrue to people who need it.

With a growing family, my mother had not much patience with this idea. Under the marriage settlement of her parents, she was entitled to some property on her own marriage but her mother simply did not give it to her. Whether my mother knew her rights or ever demanded them I do not know. It is possible, however, that if she had she might have been able to avert the calamity that fell a few years later.

The aftermath of the Irish war of independence had produced a kind of tension or jealousy, or perhaps a sense of lost opportunity, which carried with it a lowering of standards. My parents' bank manager coveted Dangan House, not for himself but for a friend and client to whom he wished to do a favour. Without giving my parents time to arrange finance, which they might well have done, the bank manager demanded the immediate return of the small loan that had been given to buy the property. My parents protested in vain. The manager ordered the house to be sold forthwith. My parents said it would take time to find a buyer. The manager said he already had one, and named his friend, who promptly bought the house, displacing us apparently without scruple, if he knew the full details at all.

This was the story I heard in my youth and for a long time I thought it was a childish version of something much more complicated and reasonable, but it was not so. In any case the house was irrevocably gone. Once more we were on the run, fleeing, tearing up roots.

Dangan has never changed: the urns on the front steps, the light gate that cuts off the gravel sweep from the avenue, the yew tree with my mother's rambler roses, the wistaria, the cobbled stableyard are all exactly the same, though a subsequent owner

The rear of Dangan House today

Salthill, near Galway

neglected the outbuildings to the point of ruin. Only the walled garden is different. That same owner – the bank manager's friend died within a year of buying the house and it was sold again – must simply have closed the garden gate and never looked in there afterwards. When the present owner started a market garden, his tractors turned up load after load of cobblestones from the totally overgrown paths. The currant bushes and raspberries were choked by grass and weeds, and the espalier fruit trees were skeletons on the high stone walls.

Barna, the harbour

FIVE

THEIR determination that their children should know the Irish language decided my parents on our next resting-place. There were other, more comfortable possibilities but, as they said, this opportunity seemed too good to miss. They settled in Barna, then an Irish-speaking village four miles from Galway, on a sandy road that led by the sea until it reached a cross-road with two public houses facing each other from opposite corners. Each of the public houses was also a shop. To the right, a narrower sandy road led over a boggy mountain and back to our beloved Dangan. The other, only a few hundred yards long, led to a small pier that had been built as a relief work during the great famine of 1847. Ahead, the road continued for fifty miles until it reached the islands. A girls' school, a scatter of cottages along the roadside for a quarter of a mile or so, and a post office made up the rest of the village.

We had two tiny houses side by side on the quay road within twenty-five yards of the sea. Each had a kitchen and a little parlour downstairs and three bedrooms above. There was no bathroom or lavatory. Commodes abounded, and there were two huts at the top of the garden, which sloped uphill, with dry lavatories of the kind we had had in our last school. One of the parlours was instantly filled with books, the other became a store-room. One kitchen had a range and the other had an open hearth on which our maids baked the most beautiful soda-bread in the world, in a pot-oven. Both doors stood constantly open – it would have been considered ill-mannered to keep them shut by day. The cottages were quite new because the Black and Tans had burned the whole row a few years before. Water had to be drawn from a well on the bog road, ten minutes' walk away, across the main road, then through a field of brambles and long grass where the water bubbled secretly out of the ground. It was important to draw water in a field where there were no cows. The owner of the field had gone to America long since and his house was in ruins, but the well kept his name alive: *Máirtín Bhairbre*, Martin the son of Barbara.

We lived in Barna for a glorious year. There were other children of our class in the village but we scarcely knew them, because they never went to the local school. Our friends were the children from the scattered cottages of the whole neighbourhood. They

were never called cottages, always houses, though none had more than three rooms. The reason may well be that the Irish language contains no satisfactory word to designate something between a house and a hut or shack.

We ran freely in and out of the houses of our friends and came to know their families. Some houses, though not all, had a welcome for everyone. If one sat quietly for an hour or two in a corner, half a dozen visitors would call for a chat or to pass on news. No one took any notice of us, or so it seemed. The conversation was mostly in Irish which we were fortunately able to understand, and so we learned who was going to America, who had had a letter, who was getting married, and whether there was a reason for it, and who had died.

We had a feeling that we would not be welcome at wakes, and I doubt if our parents would have encouraged us to go to one. But the children of the village often went, since their prayers were highly valued and naturally the first business on arrival at a wake was to pray for the dead.

The children had a selection of wake games which we played even when no one was dead. An organiser was necessary. We had one, a boy named Peteen, of about eight years old, who habitually wore his cap at a rakish slant and glared evilly at passers-by as if he were constantly expecting to be attacked. This was true, and he had a reputation for being a hard task-master, perhaps in revenge. The game began by his giving a name to each player, preferably one that was unfamiliar or outlandish or hard to pronounce – Niagara, Aurora Borealis, Wild Cat of the Mountain. Peteen took a stand with his back to the fire, facing his audience, armed with a stick which he waved in his right hand to terrify the company. Then he began in a loud, high tone:

> *The priest of the parish went out one night.*
> *He lost his most considering cap.*
> *Some says this and some says that*
> *And some says –*

He glared around, pointing his stick slowly at each of us in turn, then suddenly stopped at one of us and yelled a name:

> *Niagara!*

The unfortunate child who had the name Niagara then began a rapid dialogue with him:

> *'Is it me, Sir?'*
> *'Yes, you, Sir!'*
> *'You're a liar, Sir!'*

A long patter followed, in which Peteen's opponent was in constant danger of stumbling because there was no sense in it. When this happened, Peteen was entitled to strike the other boy as hard as he could on the legs with his stick. He took full advantage, with a gleam of pure satisfaction in his eye. Then the game began again, the other victims by now with sharpened wits to try to avoid the same fate. The last one to survive was the winner and became the challenger.

Another similar game, with a penalty for stumbling or forgetting the rigmarole, consisted in passing a small object – a piece of turf or a stone – from hand to hand, with a dialogue:

> *'Take this.'*
> *'What's this?'*
> *'A fat hen.'*

The object was passed on:

> *'Take this.'*
> *'What's this?'*
> *'Two ducks and a fat hen.'*

So it went on until the last person was obliged to recite without a stumble:

> *'Twelve bulls in a bull-field roaring,*
> *Eleven monkeys in their chimney-corners smoking,*
> *Ten blacksmiths on their anvils beating,*
> *Nine ministers in their pulpits preaching,*
> *Eight crooked crows with their crooked toes in a crooked crab-tree creaking,*
> *Seven grey mares well shod and shorn, their tails and manes in very good order,*
> *Six piggericks in a rye-field rooting,*
> *Five grey geese in a green field grazing,*
> *Four hares headless,*
> *Three plump partridges,*
> *Two ducks and a fat hen.'*

There were other games with occasional words in Irish, and some macaronic ones with a line of English followed by a line of Irish.

Peteen's mother was the only person I ever heard raising the old Irish keen. The word in Irish is *caoine* and means 'weeping'. Peteen lived in the worst house in the village. It was pitch-black inside and had only one room in which the whole family lived huddled together. The father was dead and they had no land, but the grown boys made a living by fishing and by building currachs for anyone who asked them. A framework of two-inch laths was covered with canvas, then the outside was given several coats of tar. The design was an old tradition and the boats were perfectly suited to the wild seas of Galway Bay. They lay as neatly as a gull on the water and moved at great speed.

One of Peteen's sisters got tuberculosis and it was passed on until in the end half of the family died. When the first one went, all day long the mother sat by the fire, filling the air with heart-rending cries. Neighbours went in and tried to comfort her but it was no use. Sometimes it seemed to me that she sang a few notes of an eerie tune in a minor key, before returning to a formless wail. The custom had quite gone out in this area and she was disapproved of for making such an exhibition. It was unchristian to view death as a final calamity – it would be more fitting for her to pray – but in fact she was reaching back unconsciously into a tradition so old that no one could understand it.

The games were considered a more proper sign of mourning than the keen. Begun to ease the long night of watching with the corpse, they had taken on a ritual aspect of their own. They were ordinarily played by young men, some of whom prided themselves on their memories and quick tongues, but respect for the dead was the main object. The ritual of the wake always included the provision of pipes and tobacco for the company, and of course lots of poteen. As each visitor to the wake took his first drink it was proper to say, "The blessing of God on the souls of the dead." A similar blessing was said with the first pull on the pipe. The pipes cost a penny each and could be had at either of the Barna shops. They were made of moulded white clay and were finished smoothly enough, but when they were used for a few years, as commonly happened, the mouthpiece became worn and was liable to cause cancer of the lips. Still, I remember very few men who smoked briar pipes. Clay pipes were used by some of the older women too, and tobacco smoke was said to be a cure for the toothache. Cigarettes were foppish novelties, too insubstantial and far too expensive.

When winter came, the people began to remember old stories of ghosts and fairies. It was hard to tell which were taken more seriously. At Hallowe'en – in Irish 'November Night' – a saucer of milk was left on the doorstep for the fairies, to show friendship and discourage them from coming into the house and interfering with the family.

The most common impression of a fairy was of a figure only a little smaller than human size, often with reddish hair and green eyes. Their size was important because they depended on this to deceive people into thinking they were ordinary human beings. Small fairies, *leprechauns* and *clurachauns*, were in a different class and were not much feared. It was these who kept pots of gold and could be forced to give them up if you went about it the right way. I never remember them being spoken of in Barna except to disparage a too-knowing child, who might be called a little *clurachaun*. Throughout Connemara it was still believed to some extent that the fairies might take a fancy to a boy child and substitute an ugly, misshapen child of their own in the cradle. For this reason, in the more remote places small boys were dressed in skirts until the age of five or six. Barna was too near the town to retain that kind of superstition. Still to this day no one in his senses would cut down a thorn-tree anywhere in Ireland, or dig up a fairy ring in a field. Stories existed of the fairies stopping a young man on his way home late at night and forcing him to play a game of hurling or football with them. Some said this was as good an explanation as any other for his coming home with aching bones and with his clothes in tatters, and on the whole those stories were not taken too seriously. The ghost stories were mainly of young men dressing up in sheets and dancing on the flat tombstones of the graveyard to terrify their more gullible neighbours.

Gradually the priests persuaded the people that wakes were improper and unchristian. It is the custom now among the Catholic population in Ireland to bring the coffin to the church on the evening before the burial, where some prayers are recited. The following day there is Mass before the funeral. Once this began, there was an end of wake games.

Customs which depended on young people for their survival were not so easily finished, but I think one that I saw in Barna has quite died out. It was celebrated on the feast of St. Brigid, the second of February, and was obviously a very ancient fertility rite. Several young girls made a doll of straw, the neck, waist and hips tied with wisps of straw, the whole thing perhaps a foot long. They carried this from house to house, singing a little song about the Brídeóg – 'little Brigid' – and collected pennies for sweets. But the next day at school the elderly schoolmistress beat them fiercely and told them it was a pagan custom and that they would all be damned. They were incapable of explaining that they did it in honour of St. Brigid, one of the three patron saints of Ireland, but they were put off that celebration for life.

Other customs survived better, perhaps because they occurred during the school holidays. The liveliest of them takes place on St. Stephen's day, the day after Christmas, and is still going strong. The poverty of Barna reduced it to a minimum, but the rite is essentially the same everywhere. The first requirement was the most difficult: to capture a wren – always called a wran – and get it in a cage, usually made of hazel twigs. The cage was then decorated with holly and carried in procession by a group of older boys, stopping every now and then to sing their song outside the houses:

> *The wran, the wran, the king of all birds,*
> *St. Stephen's day he was caught in the furze.*
> *Though he is little his family's great,*
> *So rise up, woman, and give us a treat.*
> *Up with the kettle and down with the pan,*
> *Give us a penny to bury the wran.*

This part of the rhyme was and is common to all Ireland, but there was another section which I never heard anywhere except in Barna and Galway:

> *Ting-a-ling-a-ling-behind the chair,*
> *My father was a wolf, my mother was a bear.*
> *My mother was a bear but the divil I care,*
> *I'll drive my sword through her guts, guts, guts.*

Versions of this custom flourish in other parts of Ireland, notably in Kerry, Limerick and Cork, in the area where these three counties meet. Here there are little hills and valleys, and as one drives along one catches a glimpse now and then of groups of houses or isolated farms which look deceptively lost and lonely. Prosperity has come to them, as to the rest of Ireland, but instead of killing off the old customs it has given them a new lease of life. Irish is spoken in those places, though English is the language of business and work, and there is a great sense of fun.

The custom of catching the wren has long gone, first of all because wrens have become rather scarce and also because people would think it disgusting. Instead, a large branch of holly is decorated with ribbons and coloured paper streamers and is carried by several young men and girls accompanied by musicians playing fiddles, tin whistles, mouth organs and a kind of little flat drum known as a *bodhrán*. One might translate this as 'a deafener'.

Dressing up is the main part of the fun. In former times the costumes were made of straw, giving the name 'straw-boys' to the participants. This still persists in Wexford, but in Cork, Kerry and Limerick the men wear women's clothes and the women dress as men. All wear masks of one kind or another – a piece of net, boot-polish or lipstick or burned cork applied directly to the face, or a cloth with holes cut for the eyes. Some wear their coats turned inside out, an ancient precaution to deceive the fairies or rid oneself of an evil spell.

The procession covers miles of country on foot, usually by back roads, visiting every house on the way and serenading the occupants, dancing and singing and playing instruments. As this place is a centre for the best traditional music in the whole country, the performances are well worth hearing and greatly enjoyed. Payment is made according to the excellence of the group, a poor group being considered not to have taken enough trouble. There can be twenty or thirty young men and girls in the group, and because of the date many of them are emigrants home for Christmas. These join in, of course, and are as skilled as everyone else since they keep their music going in all the English cities where they live and work.

In 1980 I was present at a week-long summer school for pipers held in Miltown Malbay on the furthermost tip of Clare. It is a village of at most two thousand people and has twenty-eight pubs which are more clubs than drinking-places. All along the main street one could go from one of them to the other, each time finding a new group making music, not only with pipes but also with fiddles and mandolins and old-fashioned wooden flutes and concertinas and melodeons, though these last seem to be considered too noisy for small rooms. The pipers were also experts in the manufacture of their instruments, especially in making reeds, and they conducted quiet seminars in the corners while other musicians played. The most celebrated of the pipers lived in England and had come over for the occasion. At the concert that finished the week, several of the groups consisted of families of Irish emigrants, born in England and with strong English accents. The parents had gone in search of work in the fifties and though the young people could now come back, they have settled happily into English life and made their friends there.

Each group of wren-boys picks one of their number to have charge of the money, which is spent on another evening at a wild party with drinking and dancing all night. Barrels of porter are brought in, bottles of poteen, and nowadays plenty of food also, since there is not so much drinking as formerly. Musicians keep jigs and reels going without a break, and the company dances sets and half-sets until the dawn. The musicians sit on chairs on the table so as to be able to direct operations. The party is strictly by invitation and gate-crashers are not welcome. At one that I attended a few

years ago the father and mother of the half-grown family were very much part of the fun and danced in the intervals of serving the tea and porter, as indeed I did myself.

It is hard to believe that this perfectly spontaneous fun could be transformed to become the entertainment put on in the villages by these same people during the tourist season, but one that I was at in Adare had the same charm in spite of its being a public performance. A small group of well-rehearsed young people had come over from the coast to this village, beautifully designed in the English style, which belongs to the Dunraven estate. The performance took place in a small village hall, the audience sitting in rows. Members of the group sang, interpreting the songs if they were in Irish. They danced and played the fiddle and concertina, introduced each time by an older man who was in charge of the proceedings. The audience came from every country in Europe, as well as from America. At half-time brown soda-bread and tea were served; then the concert continued with more singing, and dancing which was both controlled and elegant. I remembered with amazement how we used to bicycle for miles in my youth in the hope of having an evening of dancing and music, and how often we were disappointed at finding either nothing or else music of such a poor quality that it was small pleasure to dance to it, not to mention listen.

Various Jeremiahs used to prophesy that when Ireland became prosperous all the things we loved would disappear; there would be an age of television and rock bands and imported songs and music. The reverse has in fact occurred, though the rock bands are there too, and the man who is credited with firmly establishing the flowering of a new age of folk music, of bringing it out into the open and making it available to all, came from this same part of Limerick.

His name was Seán Ó Riada, a lecturer in Irish music at the university of Cork, classically trained in the international manner but unable to tear himself away from the deeper grip that Irish folk music had on him. His house in an Irish-speaking district some thirty miles from the university became a centre for the discovery and promotion of Irish music, and especially for its performance. Within a few years the whole country was humming with what was obviously its own authentic voice. And to our great delight, most of the songs that were revived or rediscovered were more cheerful than warlike. The notion about the Irish that 'All their wars are merry and all their songs are sad' is a myth. There are thousands of love-songs, by no means all sad. Douglas Hyde had long before published his *Love Songs of Connaught*, now known only to an élite and long out of print, but here they came again, in various versions, alive and well. The dance music is a positive torrent. Its variety seems unending, and now that people can

At a Listowel Writers' Week

afford to buy instruments there are skilled performers everywhere.

I sometimes dream of an Ireland in which all the disgusting sectarian warfare that goes on in the northern part of our country would be sublimated in music. The Orange bands, the flute players, the singers and dancers of Ulster would know their brothers and sisters in the south, there would be constant interchange between them – like a dream, indeed.

All of this is as far removed from the Barna of my childhood as if it were taking place on another planet. At that time the people were too poor to own musical instruments and it was true that most of their songs were sad. Their emigrant laments were all too closely related to their lives. One with a haunting melody was:

> *What will I do, love, when you are going*
> *With white sails flowing to the seas beyond?*
> *What will I do, love, when waves divide us,*
> *And friends may chide us for being fond?*
> *Though waves divide us and friends may chide us,*
> *Whate'er betide us I'll still be true,*
> *And I'll pray for you on the stormy ocean,*
> *With deep devotion, that's what I'll do.*

'Dómhnall Óg' – young Donal – of which versions exist all over Ireland, some running into dozens of verses, also combines the themes of love and emigration. My own translation of some of the verses follows the original, uneven rhythm:

> *Dónal Óg, if you cross the ocean,*
> *Take me with you and don't forget me*
> *And you'll have a gift every fair and market-day*
> *And a Grecian princess to share your bed with you.*
> *Late last night the dog betrayed you,*
> *And the snipe called out from the marshy bog to you.*
> *A bird alone, through the forest ranging –*
> *May you have no partner until I come to you.*

There was not a single family which had not lost some members to America, never to be seen again. Most of them had gone to Portland, Maine, but there were some in Boston and New York, too. These sent home a few dollars now and then, as well as bundles of American clothes which could be remade into things that the people would wear. Of

necessity they were very conservative in their dress, the older women still wearing red flannel petticoats with a checked apron, and a shawl around the shoulders, either white or plaid. The shawl was often lent to a child going on a message or to school, since the children had no outerwear at all. The poorest little girls came to school, even in winter, wearing only a single garment of cotton under which their bare legs and feet showed blue with cold. The younger women wore printed cotton overalls, usually with a dark-blue background and a scatter of flowers, the cloth bought very carefully in Galway on market-days and made up by themselves at home.

There was a tailor in the village then, who walked with a limp. His disability had probably decided his trade, since he could not fish or farm the land in any comfort. He made heavy handspun suits for the men, trousers and a long jacket, with a white flannel waistcoat which was usually sleeveless but sometimes had sleeves that reached almost to the wrist. The men wore broad-brimmed black hats imported from Spain, or heavy Irish tweed caps which lasted for years. For outdoors and Sunday Mass, the women wore fawn-coloured or dark-brown shawls bordered with a woven white pattern.

This was not sheep country and so there was not much spinning, but when they could get wool, the women spun it themselves. The spinning-wheel consisted of a bench to which was attached a wheel almost as big as a cart-wheel. A woven woollen belt stretched around the wheel and along the bench to the spindle. The spinner stood by the wheel, turning it with one hand while pulling out the carded wool into a thread by keeping it as close as possible to the tip of the spindle. A thread would be as long as six feet before it could be wound on to the spindle. Very fine thread can be spun by this means, the hairiness of the wool holding the thread and preventing it from breaking. The texture is pleasing and the finished cloth wears uniformly thin in use.

The only other place I have seen spinning-wheels of this pattern is among the Californian Indians, who were taught their construction and use by the Spanish missionaries.

The spinning-wheel would be brought outside if the weather were fine, and the spinner would keep an eye open for passers-by to whom she could call out an invitation to come and entertain her. But it was not a tedious occupation and the spinning songs are mostly happy ones. The women dyed the wool before spinning it, using different kinds of lichens that grew on the rocks everywhere. None of this knowledge has been lost. The Connemara pony show in Clifden in July has peripheral exhibitions of spinning and dyeing and weaving. The natural blending of the colours is as beautiful as ever.

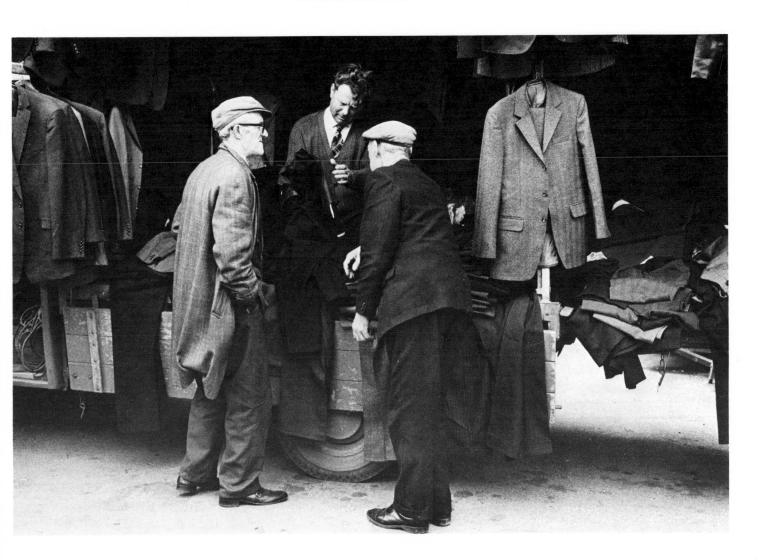

Though Barna is now a suburb of Galway, in those days it was a remote community living on its own resources. These were fishing and the cultivation of plots of potatoes, mostly for consumption by the family, but some to be sold at the Galway market. No money was earned unless the road passing one's door was being repaired. Then the men of the house had first choice of a few days' work. The lucky families had a cow. Almost everyone had a few hens. A goose or a turkey was wealth. Any girls who did not emigrate hoped for employment as maids in Galway, but they knew that those who went to America had better prospects.

For most people the poverty was appalling, and had been intensified by the large number of deaths from the 'flu – known as the black 'flu – that struck in 1918 just as the World War ended. Many families lost their only supporting men, so that there was no one to work the land. Any who were left were in constant danger of contracting tuberculosis, which removed the young very quickly unless they got away to America. Various attempts at outdoor relief had been defeated by lack of knowledge of the people and their language, and by distrust of all do-gooders on the part of the people since the famine days, when some charitable Protestants had been accused of forcing their religion on the recipients of their soup. Rescue-workers who came out from Galway at the time of the 'flu epidemic found whole families dead in their houses, and in most of them there was not so much as a saucepan in which milk could be warmed for the sick and dying.

Though conditions were somewhat better when we were there, my mother made a habit of leaving a loaf of bread ready on the table so that she could quickly cut some for any passing child. Some of our school friends availed themselves of it before setting out on the long walk home, sometimes four or five miles.

At that time the houses were all thatched, and to poor people or women living alone they were a constant worry. Straw and a thatcher had to be paid for unless a neighbouring man would do the work to oblige them. A leaking roof in that climate was a disaster. The houses were built of mortared stone with concrete floors throughout, and would have been dismally damp but for the great turf fires that were kept burning always. Since the turf was harvested by the work of their own hands they were always sure of plenty of it, and a long stack of it lay against a wall close to every house. With the kitchen in the middle and a bedroom at either side, the heat penetrated everywhere.

The revolution in housing that has taken place in the whole of Connemara was long overdue. The germ-ridden cottages could have been made habitable, but there was no time for aesthetic considerations. Some of the results are an eyesore, but to anyone who

knew the former condition of the people there is great satisfaction in knowing that they are clean and dry. At present anyone wishing to build in this area, if his income is below a certain level, receives all the materials for a house free of charge.

The hero of Barna was Father Michael Griffin, after whom a road is named in Galway. He was a young man, a curate on loan from Loughrea, east of Galway, where Irish was not spoken much. When he came to Galway he set himself to learn the language so that he could preach in the parts of the parish which were Irish-speaking. He succeeded so well that he was a loved and honoured visitor in every cottage for miles around Barna. The Black and Tans were active in Galway at the time of his arrival, and in the course of his sermons Michael Griffin told his congregation – in Irish – that it was their right to resist them, to fight back as far as possible and defend themselves and their families. Unfortunately the congregation also included the local school-teacher, named Joyce, who informed the Black and Tans that Michael Griffin was not on the side of their kind of law and order.

At this time Father Griffin lived next door to our house in the curved terrace in Galway, the house that could not be surrounded, and he was a regular visitor to my parents. With an inkling of his impending fate, my mother asked him not to use his motor-cycle as he was an easy target, and he gave it up, taking to his feet instead. But nothing could have saved him at this stage. He was called for one dark and stormy night, the driver of the sidecar that came to collect him saying that he was needed to give the last sacraments to a dying Black and Tan who happened to be a Catholic. He went, mentioning to his housekeeper that he thought he would not be back. Later that night the Barna people heard a lorry drive through the village, then take the bog road and shortly afterwards return by the same route. They went at once, and found their friend buried in a shallow grave on the roadside. Next day they took the body to Galway on a donkey-cart and gave it to the parish priest for burial in Loughrea. A little moss-grown monument marks the place of Father Griffin's first grave.

After that Barna was the victim of actions whose details, too ugly to report, I heard from my parents much later. The Barna people never spoke of them, except to say of the Black and Tans, "God help them, they were all mad."

This was recent history at the time of our arrival there. Life was improving slowly. The government in Dublin was seeking every excuse to send money and other kinds of help to this lost part of Ireland. Inspectors came and gave pensions to people on the smallest excuse – blind pensions, disability pensions, pensions for the upkeep of sick relations, small prizes for every Irish-speaking family, which meant virtually every family in Connemara.

116

Now the school readers were suddenly concerned with things we knew. We were no longer encouraged to stay close by our parents in Hyde Park. The warning note had taken a different turn and was now a lesson in the virtues of contentment. One example was a version of the ancient Irish tale of the debate between a hermit and his brother, a king, as to which of them had the better life. The king had his palace, with the newest of food and the oldest of drink and fine music for his entertainment every evening. The hermit countered that he had a palace much larger, composed of the forest trees, while his food was new nuts and fruits and his drink the water of the oldest well in Ireland. His music was the singing of the birds.

Every Saturday morning a procession of donkey-carts set out, nose to tail, for the market in Galway. This took place in the triangular patch by the Collegiate Church of St. Nicholas. It dates from 1320 and was dedicated to St. Nicholas, the patron saint of sailors, who was chosen then also as the patron of Galway. There the donkeys were unharnessed and tethered to a wheel, the shafts were let down to the ground and the goods to be sold were displayed on the sloping cart. Vendors came from many more prosperous areas and their wares were a source of envy to those who lived in the congested strip along the coast. Eggs in big wicker baskets with hinged lids, ducks, hens and chickens, wooden kegs of buttermilk, home-churned butter laid in rolls on cabbage-leaves, cabbages, onions, sometimes geese, hand-knitted socks – all sold briskly throughout the morning to the people of the town. Nearby, travelling salesmen laid out china and glass on the ground and attracted buyers with shouts and songs and various other ploys. One was to smash a cup or bowl with a loud noise, and the remark that it was better to smash it than to sell it too cheaply. The women loved china, especially if it was patterned with roses, and they groaned in dismay at the destruction of such beauty. At home their kitchen dressers shone with china and lustre jugs, preserved over many generations, washed carefully once a week.

Few could afford to buy anything but the essentials, however. When everything had been sold, the money was instantly spent on food supplies for the following week – tea, sugar, flour, salt, a few sweets for the children who had been left behind. Then everyone had a cup of tea in a cottage near the market and the long trek home began.

The market still takes place on Saturdays under the shadow of the old grey church, but now the donkeys are gone and pickup vans have replaced them. A great variety of vegetables is sold, things undreamed of by the older generation – carrots, lettuce, tomatoes, huge heads of blanched celery which grow particularly well in peaty soil.

Galway was always a considerable town, in spite of its small size. Exasperated by the

Galway

pride of its ruling families Cromwell's army called them the tribes of Galway – the Lynches, the Blakes, the Reddingtons, the ffrenches, the Semples, the Deanes, the D'Arcys, the Brownes, the Bodkins, the Martins, the Taaffes, the Skerrits, the Joyces, the Kirwans – many of them of English or Welsh extraction but with some native Irish as well. They were successful in business, exporting wool and skins and importing fruit and wine and other goods in their own ships from Spain and France. They kept the Irish well outside the walls and had no friends except among themselves, and for a long time they intermarried so much that it was said everyone needed a dispensation before the ceremony could be performed, because they were always within the forbidden degrees of kindred. In 1614 Sir Oliver St. John described the town:

> *The town is small but all is faire and statelie buildings, the fronts of the houses (towards the streets) are all of hewed stone, uppe to the top, garnished with faire battlement, in an uniform course, as if the whole towne had been built uppon one modle. It is built upon a rock, invironed almost with the sea, and the river; composed with a strong walle, and good defences after the ancient manner, such as with a reasonable garrison, may defende itselfe against an ennemie.*

Some of the 'faire and statelie buildings' are still to be seen, notably the house of the Lynch family, now appropriately a bank. One or two sections of the wall remain, enough to give an idea of its size and strength, but it was not strong enough to keep out Cromwell's army. During that terrible campaign the great families were dispersed, some of them taken as hostages, their goods looted, their precious Collegiate Church of St. Nicholas desecrated and its carved stone statuary defaced. The old stained glass was entirely destroyed at this time, and one may still see the damaged figures of angels by the sides of the windows, as in the great English cathedrals.

When I was a child living in Galway, people spoke of Cromwell's army as if it had just left. The city was besieged for nine months at that time – Hardiman's *History of Galway* gives a close account of the occasion – and when the siege was over there was very little left of its former glory. I was shown the side chapels of St. Nicholas's in which the parliamentary army's horses were stabled. Halfway up the bell tower there was an uneven wooden-floored room in which, I was told, part of the *Annals of the Four Masters*, the great Irish seventeenth-century historical document, was written while the author was in hiding there. As we climbed higher, there was another room where the bell-ropes hung down from the great bells above, and higher still one came out on a narrow parapet which runs all around the tower, close to the four faces of the clock.

From up here there is a splendid view of the little city, with the waters of Galway Bay coming almost up to its toes. The river Corrib, so smooth higher up, here becomes fast and rough where its banks were narrowed to turn the wheels of its many mills. At the edge of the town one can see the salmon weir, below which hundreds of salmon lie in the shallow water, enjoying the sun and the tickling ripple on their backs. An occasional eel passes among them, but these are usually trapped in boxes underneath the bridge. The Franciscan Abbey backs on the canal which now runs parallel with the river. Founded in 1296, it has hung on precariously since then, though it was raided from time to time and the friars driven out. Hardiman recounts that on one such raid a row of beds was found but no friars. In the eighteenth century, a complaint was sent to Dublin that friars commonly landed from Europe in Galway and walked through the town as bold as brass, and the authorities appealed for help in putting this scandalous state of affairs in order.

Near the Abbey a delightful little square houses the Court House and the Town Hall, one at either side. Everything was in proportion until a monstrous new limestone Catholic cathedral was built, one might almost say with the object of disturbing the balance of the older buildings. It straddles the view across the salmon-weir bridge, lined with marble, furnished with everlasting polished mahogany, doomed to blight the prettiest part of Galway for a thousand years. When I first looked down from the tower of St. Nicholas's, the salmon-weir and the grey stone buildings of the university caught the eye instead, in harmony and peace.

To most Irish people, the name of Galway is synonymous with horse-racing. Every year in the last days of July a highly-regarded meeting takes place three miles outside the town. During those days the hotels do a roaring trade, street musicians and tinkers flock into the town, and there is an air of carnival everywhere.

After we moved back to Galway, I lived there a long time before I realised that horses were concerned in Race Week. We never saw them – there was quite enough fun going on without them. When the crowds came back from the races the sleepy little town changed completely. Everyone paraded the streets looking for diversion. An amusement park blared steam-generated music until midnight. What seemed to me vast sums were wagered on roulette and on the various confidence tricks practised by the tinkers.

To my delight, I saw some of these in action again only last year out at the racecourse. Three tinkers composed a team for the three-card trick. One set a light wooden box on its end and covered it with an old cotton cloth, while his colleagues kept a sharp eye out for the Guards. These were busy, however, directing the traffic that began to pour out of the

Galway Races

Studying the field

Waiting for the off

The three card trick

car parks at the end of the races. One tinker spoke a rapid patter inviting passers-by to bet on their ability to spot the lady. There she was – no deception – the queen of clubs. He flicked the cards on to the table several times, picking them up to show where the queen was. One of his colleagues laid down a ten-pound note. The appropriate hiss of shock went up from the onlookers – ten pounds! It was instantly lost, but with a dogged expression he placed another bet of the same amount. That went too, then another and another, all the notes passing into the hand of the talker, who laid them neatly at his side of the box. The function of the third member of the party was to groan and look up to heaven and say, "Look at that – he'll be ruined! My God, he'll be ruined."

The tension mounted nicely, but no one else placed so much as a tenpenny piece on the table and at last the tinkers abandoned all pretence; the notes were silently handed back to the man who had lost them; he picked up the box and all three moved on, presumably to look for another spot in which to set up.

If a real gambler had appeared, the ten-pound notes would have been used as bait, he would have been allowed to win some of them and then he would have been cleaned out. But the tinkers had an insurmountable disadvantage, apart from the fact that they had overreached themselves in placing ten-pound notes. Even with the present rate of inflation in Ireland, this was too much to swallow. People no longer drink as they did, and the crowds emerging from the racecourse were in their sober senses. The main snag was that the tinkers looked so much alike; all three were unmistakably tinkers, all with weatherbeaten faces, all with wild fair or reddish hair, all with the same way of wearing their clothes, with even a recognisable facial expression.

But close beside them, while they were trying to bring off their ambitious coup, a small quiet man who was also a tinker was collecting tenpenny pieces with his trick-of-the-loop. This is a much simpler device. A short piece of rope is doubled, then curled up on top of a box. The gambler is invited to place his finger in the centre in such a way that when the rope is unwound his finger will be in the loop. But the operator unwinds a different end according to where the finger is placed, ensuring that the gambler can never win. For this trick the tinker must be small, so that he can easily slither into the crowd when the gambler spots what the trick is.

Various theories are put forward concerning the origin of the Irish tinkers. They rarely marry other than among themselves so that at this stage they almost amount to a separate race. They are not gypsies. The most common view is that they have existed only for a hundred years or so, that they are the remnants of families displaced from their homes in the nineteenth century or earlier. With the assistance of the army, whole villages were levelled then so that the land could be cleared for grazing, or because the tenants could not pay the rent.

Some landlords paid their tenants' passage to America, but most simply moved them on without considering how they would survive. If they erected shacks of sods to shelter themselves these were destroyed by the army, so that there was no alternative but to take to the roads. Gradually they acquired traditions, and several families became noted for their ingenuity in surviving and in providing for their dependants – the Wards, the Connors, the Clancys. Some of them became tinsmiths, some horse-dealers, some accomplished musicians on the bagpipes and the tin whistle.

The tinkers still have an individual style of singing and a store of songs known only to themselves. They also have a secret language rather like the masons, depending on the redisposition of consonants and the use of a mixture of Irish and English words. This is known as *shelta* but I have also heard it called *minker tarel* – tinkertalk – which gives an idea of how it works.

Many of the displaced people were at war with the society that had rejected them, and drifted into going from fair to fair with their confidence tricks, or practising other wiles on simple country farmers. I remember only twenty years ago a classic, in which a tinker sold a farmer a charm which would turn the feathers in his pillow into gold. But the charm would not work at once: the farmer had to wait three days, giving the tinker time to get to the other end of Ireland, where he was arrested and brought back to defend himself. The judge had not much sympathy with the farmer.

As tinsmiths the tinkers' work was skilful and traditional. They made a whole range of household articles – water-cans and milk-cans, scoops, pots and pans and a variety of mugs and cups. And they made the stills in which poteen was and is manufactured. These consist of receptacles about four feet high and perhaps two feet in diameter, with shoulders and a narrower band at the top like a milk-churn. Inside there is a 'worm' of copper piping such as plumbers use, to work the cooling system. The islands in the many lakes, remote mountain huts or any shack from which a convenient lookout can be kept will do to set up a still. Only a wisp of turf-smoke betrays its whereabouts. The manufacturers maintain that all other kinds of whiskey are too expensive, and that they are conferring a benefit on the community, but an unending war rages between them and the law, nevertheless. The tinkers do not make poteen themselves but since they make the stills, they know where it is to be found. In drink, they are violent with each other but usually not with anyone else.

A code of honour exists among the tinkers which precludes sexual promiscuity. They marry very young, as young as the law will allow, and have large families, all carefully trained to beg. Begging, according to a recent statement by one of them, is their best source of income nowadays. They prefer to be called travelling people rather than itinerants, the same woman said, because the word 'tin' is incorporated in that word. They do not like the association with tin, though in their day they were respected travelling tradesmen. When they could not get tin during the last war, some of them became pedlars and were able to continue their way of life for a long time by selling small articles and cloth by the yard to farmers in remote places.

One such tinker declared that he was the last pedlar in Ireland. He lived near Dunlewy, in Donegal, and found a welcome everywhere because he was an excellent musician. At the end of an evening he was always good for a concert on the fiddle, either his own if he carried it with him, or in bad weather on one provided by his hosts. A doctor who became his friend prevailed on him to stay with him for six months while he recorded or wrote down all the tunes, so that they are not lost to posterity.

It may be true that this was the last tinker who walked with a pack of goods on his back, but the tinkers of Ireland are very much in evidence at present as traders. In recent years they have taken to setting up camp at a roadside where there is a broad grassy margin. There they display all kinds of goods for sale – carpets, furniture, clothes, bicycles, old cars, tape recorders and tapes. The hedges nearby are always covered with their many-coloured laundry and a feud usually exists between them and the farmers near whose land they choose to encamp.

Irish tinkers often travel to and from England and many of them have settled there for good. When one of their number died in Ireland a few years ago, they came in droves from England as well as from all parts of Ireland to attend the funeral. The dead man was Willie Clancy, a noted piper, whose music had delighted everyone concerned with folk music over a long period. With vans and trucks of all shapes and sizes they came to Liverpool and boarded the ferry for Dublin. Soon they filled the bar and began to drink to the memory of their dead friend. The night was long and they had taken on a good deal by closing time. Closing time? They had never heard of it. Willie Clancy was dead – there was going to be no closing time until he had been properly celebrated. The barmen insisted, and managed to get their metal shutters down but the tinkers in fury wrecked the room, smashing chairs and tables, cracking the panelling of the walls, and in general behaving obstreperously. The crew of the ferry was very glad to see them totter off next morning in Dublin and take an uneven course for Limerick where the funeral was to be.

Street entertainers at Killorglin Puck Fair

It was a notable funeral but at last it was over. Back they came to Dublin and presented themselves at the dockside to travel back to Liverpool on the ferry. But the Captain refused to take them. They were utterly foiled. There was nothing to be done. The Guards were there, watching, and in any case the dockside offered no such possibilities as the ship's bar had done. And they had headaches. They sat down in groups, on the quayside, to wait it out. The ship sailed without them.

All night they waited. The impasse was complete. The Captain stood on his rights. The tinkers are good at waiting. The next day, while the ship loaded again they sat there in heaps, their belongings spread around them. Then their best possible protector arrived, a priest of the Dublin diocese who has made them his special concern. He boarded the ship and negotiated with the Captain. They were allowed on board provided that he went with them and guaranteed their good behaviour, and so they were able to return.

A determined effort is being made at present to settle the tinkers and persuade them to give up their wandering life. It is not an easy task. In the welfare state they are entitled to all kinds of allowances, so that they are not short of money. Most of them love their children and take good care of them, taking them to the health clinics so that diseases can be identified early, accepting free medicines and food and using these intelligently. The change in the appearance of the children is remarkable over the last ten years. They are no longer dressed in rags nor are they hollow-cheeked and aged-looking as they used to be. An organisation works nationwide to take care of the tinkers' problems and to assure them that they are soluble. But a very old tradition of living outside society remains to be changed, and most people hope that this will eventually be achieved by persuasion.

In general Irish people are sympathetic to the tinkers, but it is hard to be patient with the parents who take their children to Dublin from outlying camps and plant them in the cold and rain on O'Connell Bridge, to look pathetic and gather pennies from passers-by into a cardboard box. All day long they sit there, the authorities uncertain whether to force the parents to give them up for care or to allow them their constitutional rights of caring for them themselves.

Their education presents a similar problem, and eventually this may prove the turning-point. Most of the adults are illiterate. A Dillon cousin of mine made friends with some of them, encamped in a field near her home, and gradually won their confidence sufficiently to get them interested in the possibilities of reading. When she brought her Montessori equipment for the children to handle and play with, the mothers were so captivated that they ran and fetched their husbands to watch the marvel. Within a year or two those children were at school and the parents were beginning to realise that if the family took to the roads again they would be deprived of the possibility of a better life. They know quite well that, though this is the only life they understand, it is a cold, miserable, unhealthy existence.

It will take at least one more generation to solve the question fully. Settled in public housing the tinkers sometimes make bad neighbours, especially when they drink. Some have not much idea of other people's rights to property and are liable to make off with poultry, clothing from garden lines, bicycles, toys, or a purse left alone on a kitchen table while the housewife is upstairs. Some create middens in their gardens, just as they do at the camp-sites. Shocked comments come from people who have no intention of living within miles of them, blaming those who have to endure them. In fact the demand is being made on their neighbours to take a hand in settling them. Various people have proved that semi-adoption of the children by another family is a useful approach and has long-lasting results. Traditionally, the family circle in Ireland was never closed. Cousins, the children of friends, or any children in need have always been liable to be added on to the family.

The Irish climate is mild and damp. Even in winter, now and then there are long sunny spells when our neighbours in the suburbs of Dublin take out their caravan and go off for a weekend to some sheltered spot, coming back looking relaxed and content. It is possible that the most acceptable solution to the tinkers' housing problem would be to give a house and a caravan to each family. Then in summer, when nostalgia for the road hits them, as it does all of us, they could set out for a trip, long or short, and come home when they felt like it. It would be too much to ask them never again to attend Carmee horse fair, or the horse fair in September in Ballinasloe, or Puck Fair in Killorglin in July, or the Galway races.

Though Galway has become a busy modern city with full employment and a number of successful industries, the old way of life continues almost unchanged not far away. The biggest Aran Island now has tarred roads and even several cars, but in the two smaller islands one would think oneself back fifty years. Indeed, the things that Synge observed there are still true – the silent ways, especially during storms, the fear of the sea, the talk of ghosts and saints. The language of these two islands is still Irish. When the people come to Galway to sell their cattle or seed potatoes they are in an alien land, using a foreign language. As one man put it, "I am like a dumb."

Life is hard and cold in the islands. Storms can isolate them for weeks on end, though

King of Puck Fair

At Puck Fair a male goat is chosen to preside over the festivities

Time for a drink and a tune after the installation of King Puck

the helicopter gets in essential food when this happens. In good weather there are passenger planes and a ship. But most Aran people have no wish to leave. The wind, sometimes strong enough to blow a man down, is the sweetest and cleanest in the world. The sea around is as clear as rock-crystal and throws up large, beautiful shells never seen on any other part of the coast. The limestone land grows good horses and cattle, and there is no poverty there.

Time means nothing. On the middle island, Synge's favourite rock, known as 'Synge's Chair', where he sat to watch the sea, is still pointed out. Every day seems to have forty-eight hours. Everyone knows everyone else's business and children and animals. Once I borrowed a horse to ride to the end of the big island, to the lighthouse, where at that time there was no real road, only a grassy track. The horse, named Griffin, was old and tired and failed to see the point of the excursion, and after a while he began to slow down to a maddening stroll. I flicked the end of the reins past his ear to make him go faster, and a voice called out to me from a doorway a few hundred yards away, 'There was a time when you wouldn't do that to Griffin!' Everyone came out to see me pass, everyone knew that we were staying in the big cottage that Robert Flaherty built to make *Man of Aran*.

With families of ten and twelve children, naturally a great many people have to emigrate from Aran, but some of them come back when they have made enough money to live on. A few years in New York or Cleveland or Chicago at back-breaking work, saving every penny, makes the island life seem very sane and desirable. In former times women often worked as maids in New York to earn a dowry, coming back to live almost as simply as their mothers did. But when their children began to emigrate, some never to return, sadness overcame them and they aged very young.

I knew one woman who was unwilling to return. She had taken a fancy to New York and the Episcopalian clergyman's family she worked for there. But her husband, to whom she had been engaged before leaving home, set out in pursuit and brought her back to honour her bargain. He stayed six months in New York and never learned a word of English, having spent all his time with Aran people there. His wife spoke nostalgically of the sidewalks of Broadway, and the thrill of Times Square.

Nowadays the children are taken to boarding-schools on the mainland and have enough education to fit them for work in Ireland, so that they can come home often enough. The houses are lit and water is pumped by electricity. Gas is used for cooking, since there is no turf on the islands. One or two small factories operate on the big island and there is a ready market for the unique white homespun knitted jerseys that the women make. The boat still plods its way out from Galway, three hours along the bay, but the helicopter service makes it easier to find doctors and teachers willing to serve a few years on the islands. Tourists liven up the summers, many of them coming to learn Irish just as they did almost a hundred years ago. Spanish trawlers visit constantly and some of the Spaniards have married in the islands and make their base there instead of in Vigo.

The islands have produced several writers, notably Liam O'Flaherty who writes both in Irish and English. His best known novel is *The Informer*, which was filmed with Victor MacLaglen in the main role and brought him international recognition. His short stories, particularly of animals and of the more primitive side of life on the islands, have an intensity that reflects the tough, strong mind of his own people. A gentler writer, a poet who uses only Irish, is Máirtín Ó Direáin. Now in his seventies, he is just young enough always to have been able to write in the certainty of being understood throughout the country.

When Ó Direáin was a student at the university in Galway he was recruited among many others to form a part-time company of actors for the new Irish theatre, in which both of my parents were concerned. I saw its first play, a version of the story of Diarmuid and Gráinne, which was written, mounted, directed, and had its costumes designed by Michael MacLiammóir, who also played the part of Diarmuid.

MacLiammóir was a theatrical genius of a rare kind, born into the theatre, already well travelled, master of many languages, with an actor's ear, and above all with a remarkable visual talent which could have brought him equal success as a painter. His designs for costumes were little masterpieces. They not only showed clearly the texture and colour of the cloth required but also each one was a portrait of the actor or actress who was to wear the costume, transformed into the character of that part. He designed the stage curtain, black with a celtic-looking snake, which I think is still in use. Always an enthusiast for Irish, he had written his first book at the age of seventeen – four short stories in Irish, illustrated by himself.

MacLiammóir stayed only a year or two in Galway before going off to Dublin to found the Gate Theatre with Hilton Edwards. He was never parochial in his outlook and saw no reason why Irish theatre should be restricted to Irish subjects. In this he had a strong supporter in my mother who succeeded him as the costume designer; both she and my father were directors of the theatre for six or seven years. It was there that I first saw Molière, Shaw, Lorca, Ibsen, Chekhov and Granville Barker, as well as the Irish plays that were current in the Abbey at the time, all translated into Irish. Seeing them in

135

translation showed up the structure of the plays. It was not until I saw my first plays in English years later that I realised how language could seem to carry off a weakness in structure. Molière, Henri Ghéon and Lorca were translated by Liam O Briain, my godfather, a former freedom fighter who was professor of French and Spanish at the university. He also loved acting in the plays himself and though his talent was minimal he was sometimes allowed to take older parts. The Irish theatre served as an apprenticeship for many professional actors and playwrights, including Siobhán MacKenna who acted there as a student, and Walter Macken who was its manager for a few years.

Inevitably, we fell in love with the theatre just as my mother had done. My father had awakened our enthusiasm by his reading of Shakespeare, often with a part and a book for each of us. He made a splendid Macbeth and a bitter, brooding Cassius. We lived at this time in a huge cut-stone house which had once been the house of the headmaster of a school and now belonged to the university. Beyond a swinging door at the end of a corridor a wonderland of big empty rooms opened out, some with platforms which could be used as stages, some with cloakrooms where stage props could be stored, all with conveniently placed lights for stage- or house-lights as needed. Here we performed plays of our own composition, pressing our friends in to play parts, improvising with glorious unselfconsciousness our own versions of the plays we had seen in the theatre. Years later I learned that this was common practice with the Irish fit-up theatres. The company would go to a cinema in the nearest big town, come back to the remote village in which they had hired a hall, and there act out the story of the film they had seen.

For several years this free, exciting life continued. Then civilisation struck and we were all in turn sent off to boarding-schools.

Sligo

SIX

♣

M Y MOTHER suddenly decided that I should follow my two sisters, who had gone to the Ursuline convent at Sligo two years before. I reached the school in October 1931, a month after everyone else. Though Sligo is only eighty miles from Galway it took most of the day to get there by train. My mother escorted me to Athenry, where she bought me a book at the station bookstore, *Wild Horse Mesa* by Zane Grey. She saw me briskly on to the Sligo train, ordered me a tea-basket to be delivered at Claremorris, and took the train home.

The picturesque parts of Mayo all lie near to the coast. There are high mountains and wild lonely bays and long sandy beaches and many lakes. The train took an inland route, through flat bogland and damp fields, stopping every ten miles or so, puffing quietly, while the country people heaved themselves in and out of the carriages with their baskets. First there was Tuam, then Claremorris – I knew its name from Raftery's poem about County Mayo, in which he lists the delightful places where he proposes to spend the spring and summer. Then came Swinford, Curry, Tubbercurry, Collooney, Ballisodare and at last Sligo. Twenty miles or so south of Sligo the land improved. There were comfortable farms and good villages, some with flour-mills on their rivers, and the people were better dressed. The older women still wore little black bonnets tied under the chin with velvet ribbons, and long black cloaks. None of them looked poor as the Galway people did.

Beyond Charemorris a village named Knock lay a few miles from our route. Here, in 1879, it is said that a group of people saw a vision of the Virgin with saints, at the end wall of the village church. This occurred during heavy rain so that the appearance of a strong light was something against nature. The story has persisted for more than a hundred years, and Knock is the biggest place of pilgrimage in Ireland, but it was always a moot question whether the vision ever happened at all. Sceptics said instantly that it was an optical illusion; the Church frowned on it as a possible hysterical excess, a phenomenon for which there is a long history. But the local people continued to visit the site, to pray and do rounds of the church.

At the time of the apparition this must have been the most desolate place in all

Knock, County Mayo

Waiting pilgrims

The new church at Knock

Europe. The notion that there was only one famine in Ireland is incorrect. Famine was endemic. Every year or two the potato crop failed and no substitute was available. Even in a good year there was a gap between the end of the old potatoes and digging the new ones. The shortage affected only the very poor. Plenty of food was always available to anyone with money. Emigrants kept the people at home barely alive with tiny contributions in dollars or pounds. The workhouse loomed as a terror in the minds of all, largely because policy insisted that the families be separated, the men in one part of the building, the women in another, and children over a certain age in another. It was a living death, and only starvation would force people to avail themselves of it. Into this desperate community came a stream of light, the mother of all mankind, the mother of a loving God who protects the poor, Mary of Graces, the Tower of Ivory, the House of Gold, the Ark of the Covenant, the Gate of Heaven, to whom the people addressed themselves in prayer every evening of their lives – why should they not believe it? They certainly had no other protector.

Nowadays, train-loads and bus-loads of pilgrims come to Knock from all over Ireland on Sundays in summer. The visit of Pope John Paul II to the site has further increased the numbers. A church as big and as ugly as a football stadium has been erected, the parish priest remarking that if the crowds at football matches need shelter from the rain it should be proper for the crowds of pilgrims to have the same protection. It rains a great deal at Knock. On weekdays, as you drive through the village now, small family groups can be seen walking quietly around the church grounds, saying the rosary aloud. Traders of all kinds are forbidden inside. A strong sense of spirituality pervades the precincts of the church, as it does in Lourdes, as if the force of the pilgrims' prayers has accumulated over the years and converted this into a holy place. There are stories of miracles, some of them quite extraordinary, of injured bones restored and paralysed limbs recovered. A team of doctors acts as a consulting body. I have spoken to some of these, who say that at a certain point it had to be admitted that no explanation within their discipline was possible. But the general spirit of the pilgrims is simply one of prayer.

Places of pilgrimage in Ireland differ widely in their position in the minds of their devotees. No one asks for a miracle as he climbs Croagh Patrick, except the miracle of getting down the mountain without a few broken bones. Neither do the pilgrims to Lough Derg, otherwise known as St. Patrick's Purgatory, where three agonising days are spent on a rocky island in a lake. It is as if St. Patrick is above anything so childish as performing miracles. These pilgrimages are purely penitential, and the story goes that you ensure yourself a place in heaven if you get through the exercises at Lough Derg once in your lifetime.

Like Croagh Patrick, the Lough Derg pilgrimage is only for the tough and hardy. It has continued without interruption for more than a thousand years. William Carleton, one of the few nineteenth-century Irish writers who spoke the Irish language from the cradle, has an amusing account of a group of pilgrims walking to Lough Derg. The company has changed but the exercises are the same, consisting of a ferocious combination of fasting and prayer.

Pilgrims come to the lake edge and are rowed across to the island, where they remove their shoes and begin at once to pick their way on the razor-edged stones from one 'bed' to another, reciting the rosary at each one. The beds are circles of stone, which may once have been cells. No food is eaten except dry toast and what is known as Lough Derg soup, a dreadful concoction of water and salt and pepper. The first night is spent at prayer in the church, and those who doze off are prodded into action again by their nearest neighbours. The second day has another ritual of prayer, including Mass, and in the evening the pilgrim may go to bed in a bunk-house where he remains until Mass-time next morning. He is rescued by the boatman and taken off the island about noon, still with no real food, and the course insists that he may not eat until midnight that night. All the way to Sligo or Galway he dreams of food and, sure enough, the hotels are waiting for him with a substantial meal – by arrangement.

A friend of mine who is a biologist made this pilgrimage in the 1950s, and at the end of it she felt it incumbent on her to call on the parish priest who is in charge of all the arrangements. She commended him politely for the tone and the general efficiency of things but said she felt it necessary to point out that the cups used for the soup were cracked and chipped beyond what hygiene would allow. She had seen people with skin infections on their hands and even on their mouths using the cups, and almost certainly passing on their germs to others. He heard her out in silence, sitting sideways at his breakfast table, then suddenly rose up and seemed to tower over her like an avenging angel. She left the island in a daze, with only partial memories of his words – limb of Satan, godless woman, interfering interloper, scarlet sinner – if these were not his words they certainly were what he wished to say. All the way home to Dublin she felt his hot breath following her. But she felt too that he was quite right. She had attempted to interfere with the artistic effect of the pilgrimage; she had failed to suspend civilisation and education and flow with the tide of religious experience that was all around her. Things are more hygienic there now, though heart-attacks and perforated ulcers overtake the weak. But as the Irish say, it's a lovely way to go.

Other saints are more likely to be asked for miracles than St. Patrick. His way was too austere for that presumption. Holy wells abound in Ireland and are places of local pilgrimage known in English as 'patterns'. The word has nothing to do with its English meaning. It is the Irish word *patrún* derived from the Latin *patronus*, the patron saint of the place of pilgrimage. Though so many of these shrines and holy places exist, each one has its own individual personality. This is not surprising, since they are all related to people who really existed, most of them between the fifth and the twelfth centuries, whose characteristics have been remembered and perpetuated by succeeding generations.

Naturally over the years extraordinary stories have accumulated around them. I was shown the sizeable rock on which St. Declan sailed from the Welsh coast to Ardmore in County Waterford. St. Fanahan takes the form of a fish and looks up at you out of his holy well if he intends to grant your request; St. Gobnait hurled a stone so hard that it lodged in the wall of an oratory and can still be seen – these are the fairy-tales of a genuine caste of holy people who either arose from the Irish scene or formed it, more than a thousand years ago. In his Abbey Theatre production of Synge's play *The Well of the Saints* Thomas Murphy had the happy idea of making the saint a cantankerous old man, irritated with the importunities of the country people who always wanted to be cured or not cured of something or other. But in real life, when people go to their saint's well or to the little cells that are scattered around the country, it is in a spirit of pure prayer, to honour the memory of the saint and to ask in the most general way for the benefit of salvation.

At a time when everything Irish was regarded with suspicion, the clergy rather frowned on the pious practices associated with patterns and pilgrimages but nowadays they take a kindlier view. They join the people and say Mass for them, while pointing out that superstitious actions, such as tying bits of cloth on bushes or dropping small coins or pebbles into wells, are useless and undignified. Still in remote places people continue to do these things, almost as if they feared to break a tradition so old. If one were ill-mannered enough to question them they would probably say that it does no harm. A respected proverb in Irish counsels that one should neither break a custom nor make one: *Ná bris nós agus ná déan nós*.

Crofton Croker in *Researches in the South of Ireland*, published in 1824, says that patterns commonly ended in drunkenness and fighting. What had been a religious pilgrimage degenerated into superstition and rowdyism during the period when the

Catholic clergy were forbidden to practise in Ireland. Their restoration gradually brought back better behaviour, and somewhat later Daniel O'Connell succeeded in a parallel improvement by putting an end to faction fighting. This was a disgraceful feuding between families, usually ending in a pitched battle, sometimes in single combat, with long sticks or small clubs. O'Connell knew the value of symbols. He asked the people to come to their traditional cross-roads battle-grounds carrying green branches as a symbol of peace. The clergy supported him and the custom almost died out. It persisted in remote places until fifty years ago, but it would be difficult now to find an example.

There was no trace of superstition in the convent where I grew up. I have read extraordinary accounts of repression and brainwashing and mindless, lengthy devotions in convent schools, but these certainly did not exist in that place, so far as I could see. Instead there was a feeling of peace and order and quiet contemplation, combined with enough activity to keep life very interesting. There was also an air of sophistication, of learning, among the nuns themselves, not surprising since most of them were university graduates.

It was originally a French foundation, though based on the Italian community of St. Angela of Brescia, and the founders of the Irish community had come to Ireland after the Revolution. When they came to the west they settled, of all places, in the house which I knew as a ruin in the field between Dangan House and the river. They stayed there only three years before moving to Sligo, but the ruin was always known as the nuns' house. In Sligo they opened a school for middle- and upper-class children, of whom there were not too many among the Catholic population in 1806. They renewed themselves continually from among their own pupils, a compliment to their example and their warm friendliness.

The language of the school was French for a long time and traces of this remained in the names of rooms and of pretty spots in the gardens. There were plaster casts of Greek heroes in a large studio with a north light, and the parlours contained screens painted with swans and water-lilies, relics of the education of young ladies in the early nineteenth century. But later the nuns had moved with the times, teaching the courses required for the examining body known as the Royal University and proudly displaying on the long corridors photographs of their graduates, in flowing skirts and pompadour hairstyles, each firmly labelled with her name and the letters B.A.

The effect of this experience reached forward into their attitude ever afterwards. They remained passionately devoted to the education of women, and long after the

In the Ursuline convent school at Sligo

foundation of the National University made these external courses obsolete they continued to use their knowledge to give us an education based on interest and on the assumption that we would continue to learn all our lives. But they frequently referred back to the principle of their founder, the Italian St. Angela, that the most natural thing for a woman is to be a wife and mother, and they saw no incompatibility between the study of science and literature and the likelihood that we would opt for the same way of life as our own mothers had done.

It was noticeable that they never suggested that the only object of our education was to make us interesting companions for our future husbands. The idea was rather that learning was a good to be pursued for its own sake, and the parable of the ten talents was invoked to prove it. A feature of their philosophy was the reiterated statement that there was no special virtue in being clever, satisfactory though it might be in other respects. You developed your talent, such as it was, as the gift of God, and wasted no time in speculating about its size.

The Ursuline nuns were an enclosed community and remained so until the second Vatican Council. This meant that they never left the precincts of the convent except on a visit to a dentist or a distant doctor or hospital. Even then they always went in pairs. Once a year they took a house in Mullaghmore, a few miles away, for some sea-bathing and a rest from their labours. Otherwise their lives were spent in a routine that never varied. They were in their chapel before six in the morning, where they said matins in common; then they had a period of silent meditation, and finally Mass at half-past seven, by which time the girls had been aroused and were all present. All day long the nuns taught classes or prepared them, supervised study, corrected exercises, visited their chapel for long periods in the middle of the day and in the evening, falling into bed exhausted at ten o'clock. By canon law they were obliged somewhere along the line to have what is called a recreation period, where the whole community met and chatted among themselves for half an hour or so, but even then their hands were not idle. That was the time for embroidery and crochet work for the altar-linen.

All of this was a shadowy background to our activities, which began when we woke up to the sound of a brass bell being carried through the dormitory at a run by a young nun who then raced back to the chapel so as not to miss too much there. She came back in a quarter of an hour to make sure that everyone was up, and then disappeared again, and we made our way one by one in the freezing darkness of an Irish winter morning to our part of the chapel where we waited for Mass to begin. The chapel was divided into three sections, one for the choir-nuns who were educated and ran the school, the second

149

for the lay sisters who had little or no education and did the housework and cooking and answered the front door, the third section for the pupils of the school and any lay teachers who lived on the premises.

Classes began soon after nine and went on until half an hour after noon when there was dinner; then there was almost an hour of free time which was to be spent in the fresh air. Games were barely considered at all. There were some tennis courts, and though there was a sandy hockey pitch it was not taken too seriously. Our exercise, therefore, was taken mostly by walking within the large grounds, in pairs or in threes, chatting in ladylike fashion, never raising our voices too loud. We all owned hockey sticks and some went to play, if they could find the ball. Never a social fighter, I only once took part in these games and was left shivering between the goal-posts until full-time fortunately intervened and saved my life. But I missed the boats and bicycle rides and the occasional horses to which I had access at home.

Classes continued from two until four, until six for the older girls, then study filled the rest of the day until nine o'clock, when we said the rosary, in Irish, in our chapel. This was at right angles to the choir-nuns' chapel, where black figures moved in and out as our teachers, now transformed into different beings, went through their own devotions. Sometimes we could hear them chanting the liturgy of the hours in Latin, remote and mysterious.

After the rosary we danced waltzes and fox-trots to the piano played by one of the girls. These were the only dances allowed – indeed, the fox-trot had only recently been permitted, as it might have proved the thin end of the wedge for all kinds of other novelties. At half-past nine we went to bed and slept like the dead.

When I visited the convent recently there had been some remarkable changes. It is now the best-organised centre for school games for miles around. A bus takes some of the girls twice a week to a riding-school a few miles away. An army sergeant comes in to teach eurhythmic dancing, so effectively that two of the girls travelled to Poland last year to show their skills there on behalf of Ireland. Jeans have replaced the dark-blue dresses and black stockings that we wore, though some of the girls politely put on brown uniforms to be photographed. I remember the flutter we caused one year when the warm weather came in June and some of us asked to be allowed to wear short-sleeved blouses. A conference was held and it was decided that, though this might be somewhat avant-garde, it was a reasonable request. The nuns knew that people did wear short sleeves, had done it for several years. No point in being fuddy-duddy about it. And they looked nice on young girls. Short sleeves were a good idea. The revolution took place.

The school has represented Ireland in eurhythmic dancing

At this time the nuns wore a marvellous habit which must have dated back hundreds of years. It consisted of a heavy grey tweed skirt, pleated all round and reaching – of course – to the ground. Over that, for the choir-nuns only, there was a fine black serge skirt which was looped up into a series of folds and hung in bunches around the waist. This outer skirt was let down and became a long train when they went to the choir for their offices. It took years to adapt to wearing such unwieldy clothes. A novice who complained of them was told tartly by the novice-mistress that anyone who found the habit too heavy would hardly do in the Ursulines. They abandoned this picturesque clothing at the time of the second Vatican Council, the same which relieved the French Sisters of Charity of their wide white starched bonnets, but some of the older nuns miss the distinctive mystique that went with it. At the same time they abandoned the difference between choir and lay sisters, which many of them had disapproved of for a long time.

Now the school has a large well-stocked library, replacing the two bookcases which contained our permitted reading material for weekend entertainment purposes. Blameless novels by soft-headed but reliable ladies were there in rows, notably those of an Irish ex-nurse named Annie M. P. Smithson. They were far below the level of our general literacy – our teachers had seen to that – but we were still supposed to suffer them, indeed to enjoy them. I once asked in exasperation why such drivel should be in a school library at all and the nun who had charge of our physical and moral welfare replied that no girl who read a few of those books could be ignorant of the facts of life. The author had been a district nurse and was a convert to Catholicism. Using these experiences, she always made her stories include a district nurse delivering a few babies, and there was always a conversion to the Catholic church as well. Her view of childbirth was strictly from the outside, since she never married, and she tended to exaggerate the sufferings of the last moments of the business, but if one had been told that babies were found under cabbage-stalks, as some believed, that error was corrected. Her theology, as I remember, was simplistic and naïve, but it was assumed that we would be able to handle that.

The shortage of books was largely due to the general poverty in the country at that time. The depression of the thirties had halted the national growth and many of the girls came from homes so poor that books were a rarity. Still, everyone was obliged to own the complete works of Shakespeare and Palgrave's *Golden Treasury*, as well as text-books of criticism and world history, and a variety of large dictionaries in several languages. Every week we wrote essays in three languages, French, English, and Irish.

Shakespeare was the Bible of our English classes and over the years we memorised long sequences from a dozen or more of the plays, and read the standard commentaries and analyses.

Yeats was our great Irishman, a neighbour, who continually named places in Sligo and its environs with love – Knocknarea and Benbulben, Drumcliff, Tirawley, Magheraboy, Lissadell. From one side of the school buildings we could see Knocknarea – 'the hill of the moon' – and from the other Benbulben with a cairn on top, said to contain the bones of Queen Maeve of Connaught, who caused the war over the Brown Bull of Cooley some two thousand years ago. We had anthologies of poems in Irish, and the nuns who had degrees in Celtic studies taught us old and middle Irish as well as the modern language. At the state examinations we used to look for questions on these subjects, but they were not there, since they were not part of the required courses at all. We observed, however, that our school usually won about a third of the scholarships offered to secondary school pupils on the first of these examinations, taken at the age of fifteen or so.

I soon learned to take a few books from home after the holidays, and with long leisure read my way through Dante and Swift and Chaucer and Milton, as well as the novels of Hardy and Meredith and Frederick Baron Corvo. Anything I read then made a lasting impression, since it was only possible to have a few books at a time, and these had to be read again and again. In French I read paperbacks – Estaunié and *Cyrano de Bergerac* and Anatole France, and Molière, whose plays I had seen something of in Irish in Galway.

One of Corvo's books, a delightful collection called *In His Own Image*, fell into the hands of the nun who promoted the novels of Miss Smithson, and I had great difficulty in preventing her from burning it. She compromised by instructing me to send it home. Its anti-Catholic tone had upset her dreadfully, but since the copy I had was inscribed with the name of my uncle, the author of 'I see his blood upon the rose', and was obviously read to pieces by him, she agreed that in our family one might get by in the face of horrible temptation and that I would possibly come to no harm. But she did not want that book around her school. I can still hear her impassioned statement, 'You can't touch pitch and not be defiled,' and my maddening, logical reply, 'But, Mother, it's not pitch, it's a good book.'

That was the time when almost the whole corpus of world literature was banned in Ireland as either being in general tendency indecent or obscene, or advocating unnatural methods of birth control. Those were the words of the Act which empowered a censorship board to pass judgment on the literary giants of every country in the world – Balzac, Zola, Stendhal, Tolstoy, Lawrence – everyone who was anyone figured on the list. Shaw, Huxley, John Dos Passos, Sinclair Lewis, William Faulkner, Malcolm Muggeridge, Isaac Singer, Ignazio Silone, Graham Greene, H. G. Wells, Somerset Maugham, Joyce Cary, H. E. Bates – all rubbed shoulders with the authors of the grossest pornography, against whom, in theory, the Act had been passed. Irish writers had no chance at all, since they were supposed to know better. Seán O'Faoláin, Frank O'Connor, Liam O'Flaherty, Kate O'Brien, Samuel Beckett and many others were banned almost on publication, and were furiously angry. O'Faoláin mounted a one-man protest which he kept up for years, largely in the pages of the magazine he edited, *The Bell*. He finally succeeded in having a distinction drawn between literature and professional pornography. He also succeeded inadvertently in making it clear that to be certified as a great literary figure it was essential to be banned in Ireland. In my early apprenticeship to the craft I often wondered if I would ever be fit to join that distinguished company.

When sanity finally broke through, after the war, an appeal board was set up and the first crack in the wall was seen. Then one watched the papers carefully to see what was being published, and rushed out at once to buy it before the vigilantes could get to it. This was only useful for new books. It is almost impossible to explain the presence on that list of André Malraux or Ignazio Silone. In the case of Silone it seems as if there may have been representations from the Italian fascist government to have him banned, as he was a righteous thorn in their flesh at the time, living safely in Zurich.

Some Irish writers managed to avoid the ire of the censors by keeping away from the subjects that titillated them, but those who could not do this, or who were unaware that they were putting their heads in the noose, suffered more than mentally for their mistakes. A teacher who wrote a novel about the love-affair of a tinker and a young girl on holiday lost her job in a convent school in Cork. A newspaper-man who wrote about a young seminarian – not even ordained – home on vacation, falling in love with a girl in his village, was demoted from editing the literary page to counting the words in the classified advertisements. It was the last sign of post-revolutionary fervour which strove to make Ireland once more an island of saints and scholars. It was infinitely better, however, than hanging dissidents from lampposts. It must be remembered that censorship existed in England quite strongly at this time also. One need only recall the furore over Jonathan Cape's publication of the novel, *The Well of Loneliness*, by Radclyffe Hall. I remember that Ibsen was one of the banned playwrights then, in England.

The paperback revolution finally finished the question. It was not physically possible to comb through every soft-cover book that reached the shores of Ireland. Besides, a new generation had grown up and was not going to tolerate this kind of ignorant supervision. Oddly enough, the father and mother of all Irish novels, James Joyce's *Ulysses*, was never banned in Ireland. It had been published before the advent of the famous Act. It could of course have been investigated, but the omission seems to me to prove that a vigilance committee of some kind was responsible for reporting wicked writers to the censorship board. Reading *Ulysses* would have been beyond their capacity.

The Sligo community of nuns was a large one, more than seventy at the time I was there. Since most of them came from the small towns and villages of the west, they were strongly nationalist, but there were some among them who could not quite stomach the new age that had dawned in Ireland. They feared vulgarity and probably did not know that the Great War had changed the whole world, and that the changes should not all be blamed on the new Irish government. Still, even some of these went off manfully to summer courses and learned the Irish language as best they could, and thereafter taught all their classes through Irish. History, chemistry, biology, physiology, mathematics, cooking, everything except language classes were taught in broken Irish by the older nuns, in excellent idiomatic Irish by the younger ones. Teachers of French took refuge in that language. All over Ireland schools adapted in this way, some with more success and goodwill than others, so that by the end of the 1930s everyone under twenty had had a chance of learning Irish.

For a time Irish became the scapegoat for failure in other fields in which intelligence was required. If a child failed to pass examinations in mathematics which, like Irish, was an essential subject for entering the university and the Civil Service, the time spent on studying Irish was commonly blamed. Various psychologists put forward a theory that the study of Irish caused mental disturbance in children, though they were not prepared to say the same about French, or even Greek and Latin. The theory was that only the mother-tongue should be used by the child during his formative years. Some otherwise reasonable parents specified that their children were not to be taught Irish at all, since it was a barbaric language and marked its possessor as a member of the lower orders – this though it is one of the oldest written languages in Europe other than Greek and Latin, and has a large oral literature in poetry and prose dating back to pre-Christian times. Desperate upper-class parents sent the children to their own old schools in England to avoid the Irish language and to profit from the English system, as Hungarians used to send their children to Austria after the fall of the Habsburg Empire. I remember that my mother once contemplated sending me to the French convent in Holyhead where my aunt had been, because she had misgivings about having three sisters sharing too many experiences. However she abandoned that idea, since I would then have been deprived of the Irish language.

In Ireland, at present, some schools allow one to pay not to have one's children taught Irish. This is not as mad as it sounds; a government grant is paid to all schools that follow the basic curriculum set up by the Department of Education, which includes Irish. No grant is paid for pupils who leave out Irish, and the difference is made up by the parents. Very few people avail themselves of this loophole nowadays, though they would have at one time.

At Sligo, the community was largely self-supporting. There was a prize-winning herd of Friesian cattle, with a steward named Michael Silke, who sometimes showed us the cups he won for producing the highest milk-yield in the British Isles. There was a bakery from which delicious smells came, and where all the bread for the school and the community was baked, as well as a variety of buns and pastry. There was a considerable acreage of potatoes and other vegetables, though in general vegetables did not figure largely in our diet. There was a dairy where butter was made and we had as much of it as we wanted. Except on feast-days our fare was very plain indeed, but such as it was, there was always enough and plenty of left-overs. As we left the dining-room we passed a back hallway where a long table was laid, and as many as a dozen poor people from the town sat waiting for one of the kitchen nuns to serve them dinner, too. Clothing was handed out to those who needed it.

In spite of the best efforts of these good women, the monastic life was unnatural for children and brought with it an inevitable, penetrating loneliness. We became stoical, though still hypersensitive, with a deep enjoyment of small pleasures. The hours I spent playing music every day excited me almost unbearably. My teacher was an elderly Jew named Henry Franklin, whose family must have represented all the real music in Sligo at that time. My grandmother, who had got me my first teacher in Dublin, sent me bundles of music from time to time and Mr Franklin helped me to wade through most of it.

The sunny days of May and June were a pure delight, when we could read in bed by daylight until eleven at night, when the gardens bloomed with roses and flowering shrubs and the trees were heavy with chestnut flowers, when the cows moved slowly in line up the long field, their black and white pattern glinting in the sun, when we sang

Carrowmore dolmen, County Sligo

May hymns to the Virgin in the chapel every evening and when the heavenly prospect of soon going home filled us with excitement.

Criticism of their value has persuaded a great many convents to close down their boarding-schools in Ireland, indeed everywhere, and some who have kept them on send the children home every weekend. But the need for them has never disappeared. There are still children whose only refuge from the horrors of home is the convent. Children without parents or with only one parent, children of ambassadors and oilmen and engineers whose work takes them to impossible countries, children of broken marriages, all find a dozen mothers ready to love them and take care of them until they can become independent. While it is no longer true that most families produce at least one nun or priest, the Irish generally appreciate the mass of work done by nuns and know that there is no substitute for it.

SEVEN

♣

THE beauty of Sligo was an unending delight, and remains so still. If our hero, William Butler Yeats, were to come back there now he would find very little changed. One can still stand on a warm hill-side looking down over Inisfree – which means 'the island of heather' – and all the other islands in Lough Gill. Drumcliff churchyard, a few miles north of the town, is peaceful and grey as it always was. Lissadell, the home of his friends the Gore-Booths, probably has a great many more trees on its avenue than it had in his time, as the Forestry Department has taken over some of the land. It is a huge square barrack of a house, built of limestone which turns black in the rain, and even when a lively young family lived there it must have been uncomfortably cold. It was here that Countess Markievicz spent her youth. Her sister Eva was a minor poet of great delicacy. Yeats commemorated both of them in his poem beginning

> *The light of evening, Lissadell,*
> *Great windows open to the south,*
> *Two girls in silk kimonos, both*
> *Beautiful, one a gazelle.*

The misty rain is the same that contained the fairy hosts. One had better come to terms with it, enjoy it, taste it, feel it with pleasure, as it is a built-in part of this north-western corner of Ireland. As one travels north into Donegal it becomes an almost inevitable companion. When it stops for a while, the light changes a dozen times in a few minutes. A patch is brightened here and there, then a yellow-green field, a jade-green or indigo clump of trees, a blue mountain, gradually turns darker, and again suddenly blossoms with houses and fields and trees where it was a bleak desert a moment before. Jack B. Yeats, the poet's brother, used all of these colours with magical effect, especially in his later paintings which are full of moving figures from another world.

I have never been able to discover how strongly the Donegal people believe in this other world. The enormous tracts of many-coloured mountainside with wailing winds sweeping over them certainly stimulate the imagination of an already imaginative people. It is not difficult to see strange, wandering figures on the lonely beaches, or to think that the seals, with their old men's faces, might very well be drowned sailors trying to make the best of things in the depths of the sea. In the folklore, stories abound of fairy men and women luring people to their deaths, with motives either of love or revenge. The Irish Folk-Lore Commission, housed in the National University in Dublin, has collected thousands of these stories, all told in a serious manner that suggests belief on the part of the story-teller.

These deceivers are life-sized people who can speak and take the form of living or dead friends and relatives. I have only once heard a man speak of the little people as a reality. He came to visit a remote cottage in Donegal where I was staying and as the evening went on he worked his way through a bottle of good Irish whiskey, alternated with bottles of Guinness. Inevitably the talk turned to the making of poteen and he stated that at the moment when the poteen begins to run he can usually hear a gabble of little high-pitched voices coming closer and closer, until he can sense that the good people are all around him. Then he collects the first drops in a mug and throws it to them, and the gabbling dwindles as they go off satisfied.

This man is a successful pig-farmer, using buildings provided by the Government, and marketing according to the required standards. He owns a mountainside covered with sheep, which he herds with a single dog that answers to his whistle at enormous distances. His daughters work in the local knitting factory or go off to be nurses. He scorns to own a car, as there is no reason why he should travel far from home. It seems quite proper that he should slip in and out of the other world at will, since he is alternating the ancient and the modern in everything he does in his daily life. He sees no incompatibility between his half-belief in fairies and his total belief in God, though he would probably think it wrong to believe in the ghosts of the dead as evil beings. This is God's domain. The fairies, big and small, belong to ancient times when another rule prevailed. The fact that the little people are offered first-fruits strengthens this theory. I suspected at first that he was giving value for the whiskey he was consuming in such quantities, but there was a note of grudging respect in his voice that suggested he more than half-believed what he was saying.

Life in Donegal still has a distinctive pattern, different from that of the rest of Ireland. For hundreds of years it has been the custom there for the men to go to work in Scotland in the spring, leaving their wives and children to fend for themselves until the end of the harvest. They go in groups, usually to the same potato farmer, who has put up huts to house them, where they live a survival existence until the end of the season. With Ireland's new prosperity this custom is dwindling. No other way of living has yet taken

Stacking turf in County Donegal

its place – I have heard many complaints about the propensity of the Donegal people to live on the dole, which is after all a more comfortable existence than anything they had before. The next generation is changing that, with small industries offering interesting employment. The land is poor and can never be a full-time occupation.

In the old times childhood was short. At eight or nine years old a boy would be taken by his father or mother to the hiring fair in Letterkenny, where they stood until some farmer came by and offered the parent a small sum for the boy's services. There were things a child could do – herding cattle and sheep, carrying fuel, cleaning stables. Sometimes the farmers treated them well, but in general they found that they had joined the dog class and were no longer supposed to have human feelings. When they grew big enough, they graduated from the northern Irish farmers to the Scottish ones, keeping their own language and beliefs, usually coming home, sometimes settling in Scotland, sometimes emigrating to America if the chance offered.

An account of this life is contained in a book called *The Hard Road to Klondike*, translated into English by Valentine Iremonger. The author is Séan Ó hEochaidh, who is a folklore collector in Donegal. He recorded the reminiscences of his father-in-law, Michael MacGowan, who was born in 1865, and died in 1948. It is an adventure story full of fascinating detail, telling quite unselfconsciously the story of his life, from the hiring fair in Letterkenny to mining in the Klondike, until he made enough money to come home to Donegal and build a house and marry and settle down to sheep-farming. Many such accounts have been written in Irish but this is the most charming. Indeed the others, with their long-winded descriptions of the hard times endured by the unfortunate people, eventually made a stone of the heart, and became a sort of evil joke among those who had read too many of them. Since they were used as school texts they were treated with extra irreverence.

A hilarious parody of those stories, named *An Béal Bocht – The Poor Mouth* – caused great delight in the 1950s when it was first published. All over Ireland people who knew Irish were chuckling about it and reminding each other of its best parts, until some acquaintances of mine were so maddened by curiosity that they went to the trouble of learning Irish properly in order to join in the fun. The book is now available in English.

The author was Flann O'Brien, or Myles na gCopaleen, or Brian Ó Nualláin, a civil-servant-cum-journalist who used all three pseudonyms and who entertained us for years with a daily column in the *Irish Times*. He never went to school until he was twelve years old, but he was steeped in Irish folk wisdom and had graduated in Celtic Studies at the National University in Dublin. Even as a student he was a legendary figure.

In English he produced a real classic called *At Swim-Two-Birds*. This is a crazy story of a novelist whose characters revolt against his authority and gang up against him. They include the ancient Irish hero Finn Mac Cumhaill and the mad king Sweeney, whose story dates from the ninth or tenth century, and various Wild West cowboys, as well as a scarifying collection of the plain people of Ireland. One is lucky if a satirist of this calibre appears even once in a generation. Ó Nualláin died relatively young, never quite knowing how much he was appreciated. It is no exaggeration to say that he is responsible for a valuable quality of plainness and practical simplicity in our rising governing class. Anyone planning to display external symbols of prosperity or power is liable to hear an echo of his mocking voice, cutting him down to size.

Sometimes we wonder wearily whether he would have found the answer in satire to the humourless posturings of the northern diehards, those loyal, embarrassing subjects of the Crown who play out a kind of pantomime of the death of an Empire. Satire has been tried, though not by such an expert, and now it has all gone beyond a joke. In the minds of most Irish people, the present flare-up of trouble is seen as having begun in Derry. It was a much-loved city, placed on a holy site connected with one of the most loved of the Irish saints. Its name is Doire Cholm Cille, the oakwood of Saint Colm Cille, affectionately known as Doire or Derry. Throughout Ireland place-names incorporate this word Doire. To tack 'London' on to it was an old-fashioned way of staking a claim. No Irish person ever refers to the city except as Derry.

Colm Cille is said to have loved Derry so much that he decided to leave it for the barren island of Iona, partly as a penance and partly in order to Christianise the Scots. The long Old Irish poem attributed to him, but dating from the twelfth century, has been translated by Kuno Meyer and I give it in part:

> *Great is the speed of my coracle*
> *And its stern turned upon Derry:*
> *Grievous is my errand over the main,*
> *Travelling to Alba of the beetling brows.*
>
> *There is a grey eye*
> *That will look back upon Erin:*
> *It shall never see again*
> *The men of Erin nor her women.*
>
> *My mind is upon Erin,*
> *Upon Loch Lene, upon Linny,*

Upon the land where Ulstermen are,
Upon gentle Munster and upon Meath.

Many in the East are lanky chiels,
Many diseases there and distempers,
Many they with scanty dress,
Many the hard and jealous hearts.

Plentiful in the West the fruit of the apple-tree,
Many kings and princes;
Plentiful are luxurious sloes,
Plentiful oak-woods of noble mast.

Melodious her clerics, melodious her birds,
Gentle her youths, wise her elders,
Illustrious her men, famous to behold,
Illustrious her women for fond espousal.

Were all Alba mine
From its centre to its border,
I would rather have the site of a house
In the middle of fair Derry.

My Derry, my little oak-grove,
My dwelling and my little cell,
O living God that art in Heaven above,
Woe to him who violates it!

Beloved also to my heart in the West
Drumcliff on Culcinne's strand:
To gaze upon fair Loch Foyle –
The shape of its shores is delightful.

It was unfortunate that a great many of the 'lanky chiels' with the 'hard and jealous hearts' were chosen to colonise this part of Ireland. The Scots came mostly as servants and tradesmen and were staunch Calvinists. In general, over the years Presbyterians of Scottish descent in Ulster were subjected to the same kind of oppression as the Catholics, and it is very strange at present to see how thoroughly they have reversed their position.

12th July, Belfast

In what is now the Republic, similar plantations took place over the last four hundred years but since the establishment of the Irish state, relationships are far better. This is largely why we believe that the present situation in Ulster need not be perpetuated. Protestants in the Republic of Ireland compose about seven per cent of the population, a figure which has varied very little in two hundred years. Some people fear that it is going down, but this appears not to be so. Over the years the Protestants of every denomination in the Republic have found that they can live comfortably, keeping their own beliefs undisturbed, having no more grievances against the State than the Catholics have. St. Patrick's Cathedral in Dublin holds frequent ecumenical services in which all denominations join in prayers for peace. When the Protestants complain, the Catholics suffer fearful qualms lest they may feel discriminated against. It is noticeable that the closer one gets to the border, the more uncertain the Protestants become of the goodwill of their Catholic neighbours.

Long before the present era of ecumenism and dialogue, from the middle of the nineteenth century, a great many of the Anglican clergy and their families busied themselves to preserve the neglected cultural heritage of Ireland. It was in appreciation of this, as well as in compliment to himself, that Douglas Hyde, who was the son of a Protestant clergyman, was elected the first President of the Republic in 1937. Since then, out of six Presidents, two have been Protestant.

The story of the last twelve years of disturbances in Northern Ireland has been told so often that there is no need to repeat it in detail. The division of Ireland is now recognised as having been a piece of large-scale gerrymandering. The four counties of Armagh, Down, Antrim and Derry were considered too small to compose a viable state. Two more, Fermanagh and Tyrone, with Catholic majorities, were therefore added. Derry city was predominantly nationalist, and Armagh actually contained an Irish-speaking district almost on the border of the Republic. As a blue-print for disaster it could scarcely be improved. In the four counties which were predominantly Protestant, further gerrymandering took the form of drawing electoral divisions around the Catholic ghettos so as to ensure that local elections would almost completely exclude them. The maps look very peculiar indeed. Since there was a property qualification for local elections, giving up to a dozen votes to some property-holders, very few Catholics could vote in elections at all. The first civil-rights marches were intended to pinpoint this injustice.

Driving through the quiet countryside, a stranger is only reminded of the troubles that afflict the province when he passes a check-point, often empty. The farms are neat, still showing the effect of the good farming methods brought from England three hundred years ago. A survey made at that time constantly comments on the Irish habit of 'ploughing by the tail' – attaching the plough to the horse's tail instead of using harness. This was regarded as a sign that the natives were savage, and there is no doubt that the instability of life throughout the island had inhibited progress among the country people. However, it is now thought that the custom never existed at all.

The villages and small towns are unnaturally quiet. People do not seem to loiter for a chat on the streets as they do in the Republic. A great many of them have suffered bomb explosions in the ugly, random campaign of the last ten years. Most of these are claimed by the IRA, but the largest number of deaths at one time – thirty – was caused by the Protestant Ulster Volunteer Force in Dublin, when three car-bombs exploded in different parts of the city at 5.30 p.m. on a Friday afternoon, in crowded streets.

Colm Cille's Derry, his little oak grove, seems deserted on a Sunday afternoon. Parts of Belfast are in ruins, burned-out buildings, bombed houses and shops casting an extra gloom over an already gloomy city. When one escapes from the cities, the mountains and lakes are as wild and beautiful as ever, the carpet of bluebells in the woods around Lough Erne smells as sweet, the Giant's Causeway is as impressive. A tourist could pass quite unaware that for three hundred years hatred and sectarianism have penetrated every activity and touched even areas which should have been above such pettiness.

One of these was the question of the New University in Ulster. In the 1960s it became clear that provision would have to be made for the thousands of newly educated people who came pouring out of the secondary schools after the general level of education was stepped up. The logical thing would have been to extend the small college in Derry, Magee College, which had been functioning as a liberal arts college for a hundred years. It was affiliated to Trinity College, Dublin, where some of its students went to complete their courses. It was a centre of culture for the city, with evening courses and lectures on all kinds of interesting topics, and the people of the city valued it. However, in 1965, it was proposed to close it down and build a new university a few miles from the little town of Coleraine, far from all services, far from the students who would use it, far from any appropriate lodgings for them. The university was indeed built in this inconvenient place, but a series of protests ensured that Magee College was not closed down, though its functions were limited.

It must be said in mitigation that at the time when the New University of Ulster was built, there was a universal policy of placing universities at a distance from civilisation, so as to have room for expansion, playing fields and car parks. It would be impossible to persuade the Derry Catholics that any such disinterested considerations were the reason for the downgrading of Magee College. And in any case plenty of building-land was available in the vicinity of Derry.

Indeed, there was little doubt in the minds of the Catholics of Derry that the reason for this decision was to deprive them of a potentially dangerous meeting-point and as far as possible to deprive them of education, since few of them could afford to leave home and settle themselves in or near Coleraine. They also suspected that the link with Trinity College was resented, though Trinity had been a bulwark against Papists since Queen Elizabeth's time.

Ulster has a character all its own, manifested most clearly in its writers and artists. Through them and through the Northern Irish Arts Council there is a constant exchange of ideas with the Republic, as there is on social questions between England and the Republic. In fact, Ulster is so linked and bound in with the rest of Ireland through the arts and through history that there is no possibility of its ever being considered a foreign entity by the Irish. The Gaelic folk music is exactly the same, and for the folk musicians the border does not exist. To go back further, to the fifth century; St. Patrick's earliest associations are within Ulster, when he herded sheep in Antrim. His bishopric was in Armagh, which is still the bishopric of the Primate of All Ireland. Before Christianity touched Ireland, one of the great cycles of folk-tales was centred in Ulster. Hugh O'Neill, the Great Earl of Tyrone, whose family had been kings of Ulster for a thousand years, is lamented in dozens of poems of the seventeenth century as the last hope of Irish freedom. He was defeated at the battle of Kinsale in 1601, and later went to Rome where he died. His grave in the church of San Pietro in Montorio is still a place of pilgrimage for the Irish.

Every year new efforts are made to bring peace between the two elements. The delineation of the border, which brought support to the demands of the old planters, is the most difficult emotional barrier to surmount. Two generations have grown up thinking that this border always existed, though in fact it was drawn in my lifetime.

Cork

EIGHT

♣

WHEN I went to Cork as a very young bride I discovered a completely different Ireland. Physically and mentally it is a world apart from Belfast, where Sunday is a bleak day, parks and children's play-equipment out of service, no entertainment except going to church, the whole day celebrated in silence and withdrawal.

But the difference has nothing to do with religion. The Cork people are great church-goers, too. Traditionally Sunday begins with early Mass or church service and huge crowds go to church again at seven o'clock for evening devotions before going to the cinema or a dance or to pay visits. In between, all kinds of diversions take place, outdoors if the weather is fine. In that soft warm climate, long outings are possible throughout the year.

The first thing I noticed about Cork was that everyone seemed very cheerful. There was an air of stability, as there is still. The war was on, but in Cork customs were kept up and difficulties handled with remarkable confidence and efficiency. It is a little city of just over a hundred thousand, set in a river valley between low hills, sheltered from strong winds, liable to winter flooding from the river Lee which meanders through it in several channels. A large part of the city is built on reclaimed marshland. Everything grows bigger than anywhere else in Ireland – lupins and dahlias the like of which I had never seen in my life, chrysanthemums and Michaelmas daisies and hollyhocks immensely tall and shaggily leafed all the way to the top.

The Cork people are great gardeners. In Sunday's Well, the old residential area built along the banks of the river Lee, the gardens go down to the water's edge and are terraced all the way, growing fruit and vegetables and flowers according to a tradition hundreds of years old. This part of Cork was granted by Cromwell to an adventurer named Boyle, who later became the first Earl of Cork. His descendants still own the property and collect an enormous sum in ground-rents every year. The name in Irish is *Tobar Rí an Domhnaigh*, 'The King of Sunday's Well', suggesting that it was once a place of pilgrimage, but I have never heard of a holy well there in modern times. The whole area is closely built over and consists of narrow streets with high-walled gardens and many very old houses of great character. The high ground-rents ensured that these remained in the hands of the wealthy, and here was one of the favourite living-places of the merchant princes of Cork.

At least half of these are Catholics. Some time in the eighteenth century they overcame their scruples and decided to survive, and became great traders in the export of food from a starving Ireland. They were not concerned in the woollen trade, the ruin of which dragged down other Irish towns at that period. They were brewers, distillers, millers, wholesale food and clothing merchants, manufacturers of clothing and shoes, dealers in butter and eggs. The Butter Exchange in Cork is a circular building on the north side of the river and its importance is indicated by the fact that one of the town bands is named after it. This presence of a comfortable urban tradition is the greatest difference between Cork and most other Irish cities. When I lived in Cork the Butter Exchange had become a tweed-cap factory, but it still retained its character.

Bishop Berkeley, who had a low opinion in general of the native Irish, asked in the *Querist* of 1735

> *Whether it be not certain that from the single town of Cork were exported in one year, no less than one hundred and seven thousand one hundred and sixty-one barrels of beef; seven thousand three hundred and seventy-nine barrels of pork; thirteen thousand four hundred and sixty-one casks, and eighty-five thousand seven hundred and twenty firkins of butter? And what hands were employed in this manufacture? Whether a foreigner could imagine that one-half of the people were starving, in a country which sent out such plenty of provisions?*

Grain was exported in large quantities then, too, and throughout the following century and a half, while the wretched poor starved on the unreliable potato.

The Cork merchants were not concerned with economics on the large scale. They built beautiful houses in Sunday's Well and Montenotte and Tivoli and Little Island and Glanmire, with long views of their river which carried their ships through their huge harbour and thence to English ports. For the richer Catholics, the only chance of survival was a loud loyalty to England, and this they gave until the late 1940s. Then, as one of them told me, they decided that it was not such a disgrace to be Irish, after all.

They had one great virtue in comparison with the landlords in Ireland, whom Bishop Berkeley constantly attacked for their indolence and extravagance. They were rather frugal, and they attended to their businesses. They believed that education on the whole unfitted a young man for business, and they had a habit of apprenticing their sons to the family business after a youth spent in one of the big English Catholic schools for the upper classes. The Protestant business people favoured either Portora Royal School in

Enniskillen or the smaller English public schools. Catholic girls went to the Sacred Heart convents at St. Leonards-on-Sea or Roehampton, the Protestant girls to Belfast or to one of the English schools.

Until the 1950s many of the parents could not bring themselves to send their children to Irish schools. One mother told me that before her daughter went to school in England she had such a marked Irish accent, picked up from her nurse, that the mother used to pray the child would not speak in public places. In this she was very typically a woman of Cork, where everyone prays for what they need.

Under the Treaty of 1922, an English garrison remained in the two forts that guard Cork Harbour, and in Castletown Beare, farther west, as well as in Lough Foyle and Lough Swilly in the north. The Cork merchant princes made a point of entertaining the officers, until they were suddenly removed in 1938 by an agreement between Neville Chamberlain and Éamon de Valéra. For a while their former hosts felt lost, as did some of the people of Malta in similar circumstances. Ireland's neutrality during the war worried them, but they joined the Local Defence Force, the huge territorial army which was part of the country's defence against possible invasion. They resigned in large numbers, however, and joined non-combatant organisations when it became clear that invasion by any foreign power would be resisted, not merely invasion by the Germans. For me this was quite bewildering. In Dublin my Protestant friends were joining the Irish army. Until I went to Cork I had thought that all Ireland had long since been through the transition from the status of a colony to that of an independent republic.

The social life of the university had been noticeably affected by the standards of the business people. Calling cards were used, a small one for a lady and a larger one as well as a small one for her husband, all three delivered by the lady, who might come in and sit for ten minutes if she happened to find you at home. Some time after this call, an invitation to tea arrived.

A Cork tea-party in those days followed an exact ritual. The invitation was handwritten formally and arrived by the post. It was for four o'clock and one timed one's arrival for ten minutes past four to the minute. Overcoats might be removed, but all efforts to dislodge the hat were to be resisted. Gloves were to be retained for five minutes and then deposited in the purse. No husbands were allowed, not even the husband of the hostess who might be lurking somewhere about the house or garden, but you could be picked up by yours when the time came to go home. Then you might hear chortles from the host's study where several husbands lurked together, but you had to wait until later to ask what the fun was.

The maid who opened the door and who served tea was dressed in black, with a white lace cap and a frilly apron. She was usually the cook and housemaid as well, unless there was an old retainer in the family. Young retainers were beginning to disappear into English factories, where life was more exciting. There was a tradition of domestic service among the West Cork girls, who were extremely intelligent and who ran the houses with panache. They were usually saving up to get married, and a house where the maids only left to be married was considered a lucky one. I was happy to qualify as owning one of these.

At precisely half-past four a large tea was served in the dining-room, everyone sitting down to a table set with beautiful English china and old silver and glass. Flowers from the garden were in the centre. The food was delicious and consisted of numerous savouries, sandwiches, cakes and buns, quite substantial and loaded with cream. The hostess herself had prepared all of these things, with the help of her maid. One was expected to sample everything.

The ladies of Cork were magnificent cooks and their hospitality was so spontaneous and genuine that one could forgive the conventions by which it was displayed. At half-past five the children would appear, if there were any in the house. They were beautifully dressed by their nurse or by the same maid, and had excellent, subdued manners. They stayed until six, at which time the party broke up. Sometimes the last ten minutes were spent on a tour of the garden, if it was big enough.

Yachting in Cork harbour in summer and fox-hunting in winter are still the main sports of the well-to-do. Cork harbour and the ocean outside are a yachtsman's paradise, and there are several clubs. One can sail out to the Fastnet Rock or along the coast to Kinsale, which was a decrepit little town in the 1940s but has now become one of the most attractive on all that coast. The old cottages and town-houses have been repaired, there are excellent hotels and restaurants, deep-sea fishing and yachting for entertainment, and easy access to the most beautiful scenery in that remarkably beautiful countryside.

As in Limerick, fox-hunting is a sport that can be followed six days a week in Cork. The most fashionable hunt is the Cork United, where pink coats and all the other traditional clothing standards are *de rigueur*. The Muskerry Hunt, as I remember it, was slightly less particular but was also in an upper class. And on Sundays, a day on which the Protestants would not hunt, there was the Seán Peel which was patronised by Catholic farmers. Good horses were plentiful and not expensive, and foxes were quite numerous in the hilly country near the city. In summer point-to-point racing and

Spectators at road bowling

show-jumping took the place of hunting. All the byroads in those days were sandy, with a broad grassy strip at either side, perhaps designed to accommodate horses. Now they are all metalled, and the grassy strip is included to make the roads wider. One can drive comfortably into the remote corners of the county which were almost inaccessible not so long ago, but the fox-hunting is still excellent.

It is a very old tradition in Ireland and has survived in spite of every effort of humane societies. The farmers regard foxes as enemies that kill lambs and make off with poultry of all sizes, and they hunt with great alacrity. Various songs about fox-hunting exist in Irish, and one very popular one is macaronic, the English words going:

> *'Good morrow, fox!'*
> *'Good morrow, Sir!'*
> *'Pray, what is that you're atin'!?'* (sic)
> *'A fine fat goose I stole from you*
> *And won't you come and taste it?*

Then there are two lines in Irish and the farmer finishes:

> *'But I vow and I swear you'll dearly pay*
> *For the fine fat goose you're atin.'*

The chorus tells of the wicked little red fox lying among the rushes, with only the tips of his ears showing. A complicated pipe tune uses this air and imitates the yapping of the foxhounds as they come in for the kill.

For poorer people the outdoor sports are endless. When I first went to Cork, on any Sunday one might see a procession of cyclists setting out towards the west of the city, along the banks of the Lee, each with two terriers trotting alongside, one in a basket on the handlebars, one on the cross-bar, and another sitting upright on the parcel-carrier behind. A bag containing ferrets hung from the handlebars. The lord of all these animals was armed with a shot-gun, and when rabbits were plentiful he hoped to come home with his bicycle festooned with the bodies of a few dozen of them.

Beagling is very popular, and its centre traditionally was the village of Blarney where most of the houses around the green kept a beagle in a barrel. Sunday is the day for this, too, either after live quarry or as a drag-hunt, following the smell of a piece of rotted meat or fish which has been dragged across country earlier in the day.

A game much loved by young men in Cork is bowling, thought to be the game that the ancient Irish played before they invented hurling. The word rhymes with 'howling'.

It is also played in Armagh, two hundred miles away, and nowhere in between. Blarney Street in Cork is the traditional starting-point, where a group of young players and their followers set out on a long summer evening for a game that takes them walking several miles into the quiet countryside.

As you drive along, a newly-plucked handful of grass lying in the middle of the road is a warning that you are catching up on a game, known as 'a score of bowls'. It is played on the roads, a lookout going before to make sure that no traffic is coming. The grass marks the spot where the bowl fell. It is a metal ball, weighing either twenty-eight or thirty-two ounces, and is hurled from the hand as far as possible along the road. The winner is the man who reaches a given point, naturally a pub, in the smallest number of throws. The game calls for great skill, especially in 'lofting' corners, throwing the bowl across the angle to land in the roadway on the other side. Quite large bets are placed on the outcome of the match and smaller ones on each throw, the bookmaker walking or running alongside the crowd and shouting his odds at random. A favourite competition, unrelated to the game but tried every year or two, consists in lofting a bowl over the railway viaduct which crosses the Bandon road. Only the greatest champions are able to do it. The present head-gardener at the university, Michael Barry, achieved it more than once as a young man.

Of team games, hurling is the breath of life to Cork. Every village and small town has its hurling club which plays winter and summer, the better players proceeding towards the county team which may reach the semi-final in early June, or the all-Ireland final in September. This is always played in Croke Park in Dublin, and Cork's great rivals are Kilkenny, Wexford and Limerick. It is an interesting fact that these four counties are the most prosperous in the country, where the people have been better fed for generations.

The semi-final is played in Thurles, a little cathedral town in the middle of Tipperary. The day is always Sunday and the shops are closed, but the pubs do a huge trade in sandwiches to feed the thousands of spectators who begin to arrive about noon. A typical party consists of father and mother and five or six children of all ages, most of them carrying flags or wearing paper caps with their county's colours. The small boys are likely to be connoisseurs from a lifetime of parish and county matches, but the women and girls are equally enthusiastic. At two o'clock they make for the field and wait for the game which is due to begin at three. If the Cork team is playing, inevitably a section of the crowd will start up the song of Bold Thady Quill, a champion hurler of far-off days, or, as some say, a weedy little man who was being satirised for lack of the qualities extolled so powerfully in the chorus:

> *For rambling, for roving, for football and coursing,*
> *For emptying a bowl just as fast as you'd fill,*
> *In all my days' roving I've found none so jovial*
> *As our Muskerry sportsman, the bold Thady Quill.*

One verse describes his fascination for women:

> *In Waterford city there was a fair lady*
> *Whose fortune exceeded a million or more,*
> *But a bad constitution had ruined her complately* (sic)
> *And medical tratement had failed o'er and o'er.*
> *'Och, Mamma,' said she, 'sure I know what will cure me*
> *Of this awful disease that will certainly kill;*
> *Give over your doctors and medical tratement*
> *I'd rather one squeeze out of bold Thady Quill.'*

When Pope John Paul II came to Dublin, the Cork people arrived the day before and spent all night in Phoenix Park waiting for him, and still had the energy at the end of that long, exhausting day to link arms and sway from side to side, singing 'Bold Thady Quill' and 'The Banks of My Own Lovely Lee,' accompanied by the Dublin Gárda Band. It seemed likely that some members of this came from Cork.

At starting time there is a parade around the field by the two teams, carrying their hurleys, which are like hockey-sticks but heavier and with a wide blade. The teams consist of eleven men each. They are preceded by a pipe band, dressed in kilts and led by a pipe major twirling and tossing his six-foot staff. The army band-uniform consists of a saffron kilt with a green jacket, a flowing saffron cloak held in place on one shoulder with a large brooch, and black buckled shoes. Civilian bands have similar uniforms, often in shades of green. The army band may also be heard at the Dublin Horse Show in August. They play Irish marches, all of which have powerful associations for their listeners. The last time I heard them I thought they were chosen with great subtlety; the more warlike ones to urge on the Irish jumping team; somewhat more polite ones to celebrate the parade of the English team; those beloved by the German bandmaster who trained the Irish army bands in the 1920s for the Germans; those connected with the Rising of 1798, when the French sent an expeditionary force to Ireland, for the French.

When the match is about to begin, a stranger might be astonished to see an elderly cleric being escorted on to the field and going through a process rather like inspecting a

guard of honour. Then he is handed the ball, which he throws in among the players, afterwards quickly scurrying off the field to a place of safety on the sideline. This custom is observed at Gaelic football matches also and its origin is in the nineteenth century when the Gaelic Athletic Association received tremendous support from the Catholic clergy, who saw in it a chance of rehabilitating the despairing people.

Nationalism grew through the G.A.A. clubs, alongside pride in the parish and the county. They welded the people together in the same way as the Gaelic League did, and to this day memories of the sports enjoyed with like companions have a large part in bringing home Irish exiles to live and work in their own villages. This power is so well recognised that politicians seeking office cultivate the support of the leaders of the G.A.A., who in their turn feel that they carry the responsibility for the nation's integrity. A side-effect is that there is little or no ungentlemanly behaviour on the field.

The power of the G.A.A. is also recognised by some people who do not subscribe to the idea of a nationalist Ireland. My father belonged to the County Club in Galway in the 1950s. Going in one evening for a quiet drink on the way home, he found two old county gentlemen sitting forlornly in the bar, sipping drinks which had been provided in a hurry by one of the maids. The barman, the porters, the concierge were all missing, they said – gone to an I.R.A. match. My father said gently that it was a G.A.A. match, not an I.R.A. match, but one of the old chaps said testily, 'It's all the same.'

The strong individuality of the people of Cork on all levels has naturally produced a range of artists in every field, some of them well known internationally. James Barry and Daniel Maclise, the painters, were both Corkmen. Barry's picture of Lear and Cordelia was familiar to me from childhood, as it hung in my grandfather's dining-room, but most of his work is in foreign galleries.

Cork is at present most celebrated for its writers. Living there I became aware of the true basis of the work of Seán O'Faoláin and Frank O'Connor, in the word-consciousness of the people in both city and county. The Cork people have a genius for seeing the ridiculous and for inventing nicknames and using phrases that cut solemnity down to size. They take liberties with language, converting words to a different form at will. The Butter Exchange Band is the Butthera, Patrick Street is Pana, the Western Road is the Wesy, to 'wax a gaza' means to climb a gas-light pole. The rhythms of their speech flow on to a natural cadence and they use this gift to sum up people and situations.

One instance of this was when I expressed misgivings about an old lady who I thought might have fallen on hard times. 'Not at all,' I was told. 'That one has her confir money.' It is the custom in Cork for children to visit all their relations on the day of their confirmation, wearing their white dresses or snappy grey suits, and to be given a present of money by each. The suggestion was that the old lady was so thrifty that she had saved hers up for her old age. James Joyce's father was a Corkman and a great deal of the language of *Ulysses* is traceable to Cork.

It may be the propensity towards levelling that gives the impression that the Cork people are not proud of their artists, especially their writers. The first time that I spoke warmly and appreciatively of Seán O'Faoláin and Frank O'Connor I was met with a cold stare, then an equally cold question as to whether I was a liberal. This meant a person of loose ethical standards, and it soon became clear that the two eminent sons of Cork were considered something of a disgrace. They had cut very near the bone, of course, and they had dealt with the taboo subject of sex, though never explicitly. They had demystified the clergy and had shown up the falsity of some of their fellow citizens' attitudes, their tolerance of the sins of their friends, their cruelty in rumour and gossip, their sharpness in business, their ignorance of the outside world, their self-satisfaction with their own way of life, and their unconscious humour in all kinds of easily recognisable situations. It was not to be tolerated. On one occasion some of his old comrades of the I.R.A. solemnly court-martialled and condemned Seán O'Faoláin for an unwelcome short story about an episode in their fight for Irish freedom. Their feeling of insult was increased by the fact that both O'Faoláin and O'Connor had gone off to live in Dublin, the rival capital of Ireland.

Both of them had been protégés of Daniel Corkery, a primary-school teacher who had written one or two volumes of short stories and a novel, as well as a study of John Millington Synge and *The Hidden Ireland*, about the eighteenth-century Irish lyric poets. He was an admirer of Chekhov and Turgenev and saw the similarity between the Russia they described and the slow-moving, frustrating Cork that he knew. He also had a remarkable capacity for spotting a real artist and for saying and doing the right things to make talent flower.

Another of his protégés was the sculptor, Séamus Murphy, who might have drawn the same resentment directed at creative artists, if he had not had an exceptionally lovable character and spent his entire working life in Cork. He was apprenticed as a stone-cutter at the age of fourteen, and he described his life and his companions in the trade in a book called *Stone Mad*. Corkery encouraged him to go to the Crawford Municipal School of Art where he learned design and painting. This school was founded and heavily endowed by a member of a brewing family named Crawford, and has a charming position on a little square close by the Opera House. Its charm is destroyed by

the fact that the square is used as a car-park, but at night its atmosphere returns. The planners of Cork have not so far come to terms with the need for quiet spaces in their city.

Corkery was himself a talented water-colourist and Séamus Murphy often joined him on painting-trips when he was a young man. The School of Art, through the Gibson Bequest, gave him a scholarship to go to Paris, the sum of five pounds a month, which was considered enough for a student in those days. He starved on it, though he ate mostly potatoes, staying in bed to conserve his energy when his money ran out and when he could no longer bring himself to accept the charity of his better-off friends. In Paris he met an international group of students and learned enough about the requirements of an artist's life to last him through all his years at home in Cork.

Séamus Murphy loved his city and the little towns around it, Cóbh at the harbour mouth and Youghal and Bandon and Macroom and Dunmanway and Millstreet, each with its own distinctive character. He raged at the philistinism of the planners who sought to modernise all this tradition out of existence, and he drew around him a circle of friends and acquaintances who began to respect and wish to preserve the old buildings and monuments that give Cork its character. One among many such occasions was when he discovered that the City Manager, an almost all-powerful official, was planning to destroy the Berwick fountain on the Grand Parade and concrete the space to make a pedestrian island. In the days before protests, we all protested under his instructions, and the project was abandoned.

Above all he provided a climate in which artists in his own and other disciplines could relax, and his house was a haven from the solid practicality of the strong-minded citizens of Cork. But he had no quarrel with them. He loved to feel himself part of the life of the city and he always tried to join in the traditional Saturday afternoon promenade in Patrick Street, the city's main street.

Very little of his work is to be seen in Cork city churches. Some of the clergy, who should have been his most useful patrons, objected to his independent attitude. This was all the more difficult to understand since he was a churchgoer all his life. However, he acquired a patron in the person of an equally independent Cork manufacturer, William Dwyer, who commissioned him to build a church as a memorial to his daughter. This church is at Blackpool, not far from the Dwyer factory, and contains several examples of Séamus Murphy's statuary.

Some of his best work is now on permanent display in the Fitzgerald Park, a small, pretty park near the university, on the banks of the river, looking across at Sunday's

Séamus Murphy's St. Gobnait

Well, but to see it in its proper setting one should go to the village of Ballvourney, thirty miles west of Cork, where a statue of St. Gobnait stands on the site of the saint's sixth-century cell. The face and figure are of a kind that Séamus Murphy loved and are in essence portraits of his wife, Mairéad, herself the daughter of an enormously talented sculptor, Joseph Higgins, whose work may be seen in the Crawford Gallery. The strong features and jutting chin, the tall, looming figure, dressed in a Munster cloak, nevertheless has something grandmotherly about it, as if the saint knows her responsibilities and can be relied on to fulfil them. She is standing on a beehive, one of her symbols, and a bee is crawling out of the entrance to the hive, low down on the left-hand side, towards the back. This was done in a moment of exuberance, as the sculptor told me at the time, perhaps in the same spirit as the medieval stone-carvers put tiny faces or figures high on a church wall, a private joke of the craftsman when he has finished the solemn pillar at which his employer put him. One may see these, among other places, in Holy Cross Abbey in Tipperary and in Jerpoint Abbey in County Kilkenny.

Séamus Murphy's St. Brigids have the same classic lines as his St. Gobnait, though the character is different. One stands over the main door of Bantry church, and one, flanked by the twelve apostles, over the door of St. Brigid's church in Van Ness Avenue in San Francisco. Perhaps his masterpiece is the St. Patrick, a head in limestone, which is in the library of St. Patrick's College in Maynooth. The drooping eyelids suggest a world-weary but still vigorous man who is prepared to keep pounding out his message until the last Irishman is safely rescued from the devil.

Séamus Murphy was a typical Corkman in his closeness to nature and the country-side that surrounds the little city. His favourite summer walk with his young son took them to a pub called the Fox and Hounds, over the hill above St. Luke's Cross. Here one evening a boy came in with two fox cubs which he had found, and which he proposed to sell to one of the hunt clubs for rearing. Séamus instantly bought the cubs for ten shillings, took them home and established them in the back garden in an enclosure of wire netting. Thereafter, he and the small boy were a common sight with the cubs on dog-leads, accompanied by the family black labrador, on walks to the Fox and Hounds. The wild independence of the foxes fascinated him, and struck a chord within himself which demanded to be listened to. But the cubs grew up, and began to burrow, and had to be released at last into a wildlife reservation, carefully chosen, where they may be living still.

Apart from its prosperity, Cork city differs from the other cities of Ireland in having for a long time had second-level education available to all classes. In theory education

191

Thank offerings to St. Gobnait

was provided for the poor in Ireland by charter schools, but contemporary accounts of these show their inadequacy both in education and in the physical care of the children. The purpose of the schools was to educate the poor away from popery and from their savage ways, teach them English and apprentice them to masters and mistresses of the Protestant faith.

Smith's *History of Cork*, published in 1750, gives an ecstatic account of the provision made for the children in the Bluecoat School, near St. Mary Shandon church. He describes their diet and their hours of work, and the building in which they lived, which I remember as having a figure of a boy and a girl in eighteenth-century dress on either gate-post. These have since been removed. They were known in Cork as Bob and Joan, two unlikely names for Irish children, and represented in this also the ideal condition to which the natives were to be led.

However, a report presented in 1791 describes the charter-school children as 'dirty and half-starved', 'having the itch', 'half-naked', 'in rags', and exploited by thieving schoolmasters and schoolmistresses. Even without these failures, there were not enough schools, and children roamed the streets and took to thieving on their own account at an early age. Inducements to Catholic parents to send their children to the charter schools included the promise that they would be cared for, but soon only the more thoughtless parents would agree to part with their families to such an ugly prospect. In the end, only about two thousand were provided for in the whole country.

About the middle of the eighteenth century a remarkable Cork woman named Nano Nagle set up an organisation for collecting the children of the poor and teaching them, first in her own cottage and then in various wretched hovels throughout the city. From this movement grew the religious congregation known as the Sisters of the Presentation, which now has branches all over the world. Nano Nagle's work was supported by several members of the entirely Protestant Corporation of Cork. Two infirmaries had been founded for the poor, the North in 1719 and the South in 1722, and she and her Sisters were authorised to visit the sick in both hospitals. At this period it was an offence to teach the Catholic faith, and the nuns wore ordinary dress and kept a very low profile indeed. Priests were constantly being accused of urging allegiance to the king of France, and one Father Sheehy was actually hanged in 1766 for this crime. A supposed murder was added as a makeweight but, to the embarrassment of all, the victim turned up alive and well soon afterwards and outlived his supposed assassin by twenty years. Still, various members of the Cork Corporation saw and appreciated the results of Nano Nagle's work in clearing the streets of begging children, and gave her considerable encouragement to continue.

Nano Nagle came of a Norman family and perhaps she knew how to handle her own kind. Besides, she had inherited money through her uncle, Joseph Nagle, a clever lawyer who had been admitted to Gray's Inn in 1696 and devoted his life to circumventing the Irish penal laws against Catholics. He lost some of his own property under the law that a practising Catholic could not own land, but he retained enough of it to hand it on legally to his nephews and nieces. He found a loophole in the law which said that Catholics could not inherit under a will, and Nano Nagle found herself the beneficiary of a trust fund.

It was she who induced the Ursulines to send some nuns to Ireland, and their first establishment, a school for young ladies, was set up in Cork in 1772. These Ursulines were all Irishwomen, who had entered the convent in the rue Saint Jacques in Paris, and part of their work was to help Nano Nagle with her schools for the poor.

Encouraged by Nano Nagle's dogged persistence, a young businessman named Edmund Rice started a similar scheme for boys in Waterford, and this grew into the congregation of the Irish Christian Brothers. By 1810 they had begun to establish schools for boys in Cork. In the meantime a congregation of Presentation Brothers had been founded in Cork, so that ever since the nineteenth century the city was well supplied with schools on all levels.

The Irish Sisters of Charity and the Congregation of the Mercy nuns, both primarily concerned with nursing, also have schools for girls in Cork City.

Long before secondary education became common, one noticed that every Cork tradesman had had at least a few years of it and had been introduced to the pleasures of poetry both in Irish and English. An amateur Shakespeare company existed in the North Parish, presided over by a curate there. The Cork Opera House, a nineteenth-century baroque structure full of red velvet and gold paint, had a highly critical audience both for plays and for the visiting opera companies. This building was burned down in the 1950s and with it departed a tradition that was a sad loss to Cork. It was the same kind of tradition that exists in Parma, where the company in the gods entertains itself and everyone else by singing the arias from the opera about to be performed, while waiting for the curtain to go up. A new theatre was built, still named the Cork Opera House, but it has forced Cork into a modern age that does not quite suit it. Home-produced shows, theatre, ballet and opera, and the variety shows still beloved by the Cork people get no support from the cold modern building which is functionally so much better than the old one.

Cork has turned its exuberance into other channels, however. Every year there is an international choral festival, with competitors from all over the world, and a very high standard indeed. This takes place in May and is accompanied by exhibitions of folk-dancing from the competing countries, and the Cork choirs compete with the best of them. The spirit behind this, as with everything musical in Cork, is the recently-retired professor of music at the university, Aloys Fleischmann, whose father came from Bavaria early in the century as choir-master and organist at the Catholic cathedral.

It is no wonder, then, that Cork is the centre of a large area in the south of Ireland which regards it as a capital city. It well deserves that reputation, since it somehow manages to enjoy most of the benefits of provincialism without too many of its drawbacks. Intelligent, hardworking, inventive, the Cork people form a core of common sense and hard-headed awareness of their part in the development of the country. They are strongly nationalist, though disapproving of violent ways of achieving nationality until all others have been tried.

Cork suffered greatly from the Black and Tans, who murdered the Lord Mayor of Cork, burned a large part of the city centre and later boasted of their deed by wearing burned corks in their cap-bands, but in general the Cork people have put all these old grievances behind them. Still, they sympathise from personal experience with the harassed Catholics of Ulster and, while disapproving of the I.R.A. campaign of violence, they can understand very well how this came about.

The Cork people are at home everywhere, observant, sharp-witted, good-humoured, capable of long silences but enjoying conversation for its own sake, above all supremely confident of their power to charm and outmanoeuvre bureaucratic or other opposition to any of their business plans. Their hospitality is a legend, and extends to friends and strangers alike.

A few miles west of the city one is back in the deep country. The river Lee wanders along, opening out into an artificial lake with a dam near Carrigrohane, on the left bank. On the opposite bank, taking the road through Ballincollig – the 'Town of the Cock' – presently one comes to Kilcrea Abbey on the left, a hundred yards off the road, beside a full-running stream. Opposite it is the ruin of Kilcrea Castle, probably once the home of the donor of the monastic lands. The abbey must have been an important one, as the monastery adjoining the church has a large cloister surrounded by the remains of a two-storey building. The church and monastery are in ruins, destroyed by Cromwell's army, and, as with other churches with the same history, the people took to burying their dead inside.

Here is the tomb of Arthur O'Leary, a colonel in the Austrian army who died in 1773.

His epitaph can be dimly discerned:

LO, ARTHUR LEARY, GENEROUS, HANDSOME, BRAVE,
SLAIN IN HIS BLOOM, LIES IN THIS HUMBLE GRAVE.
DIED MAY 4TH, 1773, AGED 26 YEARS.

He is remembered still for two reasons, first for being a baiter of the landed ascendancy and a defier of the penal laws, and secondly for the long lament composed for him by his wife. She was Eileen O'Connell from Derrynane, the aunt of Daniel O'Connell the politician. The O'Connells were a powerful family, with an immense mountainy estate in Derrynane in Kerry, from which they constantly smuggled goods and people to and from France and Spain. They spoke French and English well, but their main language was Irish and this is the language of the lament.

It is said that Eileen O'Connell composed it within two or three days of her husband's death. He had gone to Europe as a boy and came back to Ireland after the War of the Austrian Succession. In Europe he had mixed on equal terms with the aristocracy, and perhaps he did not realise how deadly were the Irish penal laws against Catholics. He moved into his own house in Rath Laoich, not far from Macroom, and married Eileen O'Connell, who had fallen in love with him when she saw him one day in the town, dressed in all his foreign finery, as she describes in the opening lines. The translation is my own.

My love forever!
The day I first saw you
At the end of the market-house,
My eye observed you,
My heart approved you,
I fled from my father with you,
Far from my home with you.

My friend forever!
My mind remembers
That fine spring day
How well your hat suited you,
Bright gold banded,
Sword silver-hilted —
Right hand steady —

> *Threatening aspect –*
> *Trembling terror*
> *On treacherous enemy –*
> *You poised for a canter*
> *On your slender bay horse.*
> *The Saxons bowed to you,*
> *Down to the ground to you,*
> *Not for love of you*
> *But for deadly fear of you,*
> *Though you lost your life to them,*
> *O my soul's darling.*

In wearing his sword in public Arthur O'Leary was breaking the law for Catholics. Furthermore, he owned good horses, and had the temerity to race them against those of the landed gentry. O'Leary's horse won a race, and a man named Morris demanded it from him for the price of five pounds, the legal limit to be paid for any horse owned by a Catholic. O'Leary refused, and fled on the horse. Morris called out the army from Macroom in pursuit and they all hunted him down. His whereabouts were betrayed by a man named Cooney. He crossed the river somewhere near Carriganima – an old woman in the district pointed me out the exact spot – and stood there mocking his pursuers, evidently thinking that he was out of range. But he was not, and he was shot and died on that spot.

Eileen O'Connell's family pride shows throughout the poem. She names her own and her husband's genealogies, and repeatedly compares his fine appearance and elegant clothes with the poor show made by his assassins. The impact of this incident may be gauged by the fact that the lament remained in the oral tradition until fifty years ago. Like a ballad, it had undergone various changes with repetition, and a definitive edition was made in 1960 by Seán Ó Tuama, who is now professor of Irish literature at the university in Cork. One is constantly struck by the naming of places – 'Gold-appled Capling', 'Great Derrynane', 'Guagán of the saint' – a litany intended to demonstrate the importance of the two afflicted families.

At the time of which she wrote, this whole area was quite closely populated by tenant farmers and labourers, but now there are huge farms and pretty, well-kept villages several miles apart. A competition has encouraged conservation and neatness, and made the people of the small towns conscious of their beautiful surroundings. Well-off

farmers live in the big country houses that one sees at the tops of the long avenues, formerly owned by landlords who were largely absentees. The Land Commission compulsorily acquired any land which was not being worked.

Thursday is the farmers' day for shopping in Cork, and I remember their fur-coated wives fortifying themselves with tea and large cream-cakes in Thompson's restaurant before going home. They came up from the edge of poverty to confident prosperity in one generation. They believe in educating their children and usually leave the farm to the son or daughter who is most interested in working it, making doctors and engineers and teachers and nurses and businessmen of the rest of their large families.

Matchmaking was always common among the Cork farmers. Traditionally, every year a Farmers' Ball was held in the Imperial Hotel in Cork, after the harvest was in. Hundreds of young men and women from the big farms came with their parents, who sat at one end of the long Clarence Hall, watching the dancing and making plans with each other. There was nothing apologetic about this. Their own parents had made matches for them and they were generally grateful for it. The girl did not feel in the least humiliated, since she would be a property-owner when her father conferred her dowry on her, of cows and money. The tradition is so strong that I heard of an occasion when a laboratory porter demanded repayment for broken beakers and test-tubes from a large-boned farmer's daughter at the university, and she replied scornfully, 'What do I care for your beakers and your test-tubes, and my father having a hundred cows?'

Matchmaking among the small farmers is on a starker scale, and the dowry brought in by the new wife is often given to her husband's sister to get a husband for her. This could mean that the money is never spent, which is why cows are usually given as well. Cork is dotted with creameries and the small farmers rely on milk as the mainstay of the family.

After Macroom, the land is poorer. Following the river Lee, one goes by the edge of a large marsh, the Geeragh, now part of the great hydro-electric scheme whose dam is close to Cork. The Geeragh never flooded properly, and rushes and humps of forlorn land stick up here and there. Further on there are several small lakes in a chain that stretches from Inchigeela to Ballingeary.

Ballingeary village, only a mile or two from the Pass of Keimaneigh – the 'Deer's Leap' – has been a centre for the study of Irish for almost a hundred years. Some of the most eminent Irish scholars of the world have made their first acquaintance with spoken Irish there. Going towards the Pass, after a mile or two there is a turn off to the right and a wriggling, narrow road leads to Gougane Barra and the Valley of Desmond, surely the

Near Kenmare, County Kerry

most beautiful valley in all Ireland.

A large part of the valley floor is covered by a lake, and beyond it is the source of the river Lee. It trickles along as a narrow stream from the far end of the valley, now entirely planted with trees by the Forestry Department. When I saw it first it was bleakly empty, often filled with misty rain, the mountains around it ribbed with white waterfalls that drop almost directly from the summit. There are two small hotels on the lake shore, at the entrance to the valley, owned by two families named Cronin, and right before their doors is the causeway that leads to the tiny island on the lake where St. Finbarr had his cell in the sixth century. His name was Luan, Finn Barr – 'fair-head' – being a nick-name. His pattern day is in late June, when the island is thronged with pilgrims from the whole area between Macroom and Bantry.

Beyond the Pass of Keimaneigh lies Bantry Bay, washed by the Gulf Stream, so that the vegetation is sub-tropical and the sea-water feels warm. It evidently pleases the many seals that sit on the rocks near Glengarriff, sunning themselves, taking little notice of the boats that chug past on their way to Garnish island. The island is a national park and is cultivated with exotic shrubs and flowers. Glengarriff is the last outpost of civilisation before one goes farther west to the high mountains and the long, splayed-out peninsulas of Kerry.

This above all parts of Ireland is where foreigners love to settle, especially country-bred English people. Their in-built stability protects them from loneliness and they get on well with the country people. The Germans tend to be more possessive about their property and less sensitive to local customs. Perhaps they are hampered by the problems of language. There have been difficulties about ancient rights of way and foreshore rights, but over the years these have become better protected by the local councils and ill-feeling is avoided.

When strains build up, even people whose language has been English for generations tend to resort darkly to Irish. In a West Cork pub not long ago, a countryman objected to two Englishmen singing mildly smutty songs in the presence of a lady. He retaliated by singing a very rude patriotic song in Irish, which he dedicated to me, and left me with the embarrassing task of explaining the song as politely as I could to the foreigners.

The Cork people in their superiority say of Kerry that St. Patrick never went there, that he stood on a mountain-top near Kanturk and said, '*Beannaím i bhfad siar sibh*' – 'I bless you from a distance.' This, they say, is why the Kerry people have a wild streak in them, never quite tamed by Christianity. They were somewhat tamed by poverty, however, but their heartier spirit saved them from the total depression that took hold of Connemara.

All classes produced scholars and poets, as they do still, and Kerry was the last part of Ireland which took responsibility for the wandering poets and gave them the respect that was their due by long tradition. A monument to the four great poets of Kerry stands in Killarney town, unfortunately caged in by railings but still a proper tribute to its long literary tradition.

Throughout Ireland, it is noticeable that the places where Irish is spoken are usually the most remote and have the poorest land. The Dingle peninsula is a case in point. It is so wild and desolate that the Irish way of life persisted there long after it had been destroyed everywhere else. Dingle, halfway along the bay, is still largely Irish-speaking and so are most of the tiny villages to the west of it, Gráig and Ballydavid and Ballinskelligs and Dunquin. A mile or so offshore from Dunquin is the Blasket Island, where people fled during the great famines of the nineteenth century to escape the potato blight. They never settled there, though they learned some island skills, and in the 1940s they petitioned the government to resettle them on the mainland.

The success of their plea was regretted by many who did not have to endure the wild winters there, because the island had produced three folk writers, and had been the resort of Irish scholars for fifty years and more. Two of the writers, Thomas O'Crohan and Peg Sayers, had in fact dictated their memoirs but this does not detract from their artistry and authenticity. Both give autobiographical accounts of life on the island, and in the case of Peg Sayers, of her earlier experiences on the mainland as well. They are delicate evocations of a hard life in which the bright patches were sharply enjoyed. Above all the two had the gift of story-telling and they were expert in evoking an incident by means of conversation and description. Peg Sayers' account of her match-making with an islandman is unforgettable. These works are available in translation.

The third writer, Maurice O Sullivan, composed a book called *Twenty Years a-Growing*, about his life as a child in the workhouse in Dingle and later on the Blasket Island when he was taken home by his father and grandfather. The translation was lovingly done by an Oxford scholar and is alive with humour and the spirit of the island.

This part of Kerry contains fascinating glimpses of Ireland's Celtic past. At the summit of Slea Head, on the road that leads down to Dunquin, there is a whole village of beehive huts on the mountainside near the road. Who lived in those huts, who built them? Shaggy little Celtic ghosts peer out of the doorways, voices of invisible children laugh quietly, just out of sight, as you move among the tiny stone houses. Or was it a

In the Dingle peninsula, County Kerry

Mount Brandon, County Kerry